Going the Extra Mile

Adventures with God
in Seventy-Five Countries

by Norval Hadley

℔B

BARCLAY PRESS
Newberg, OR 97132

Going the Extra Mile
Adventures with God in Seventy-Five Countries

Barclay Press, Inc.
Newberg, Oregon
www.barclaypress.com

ISBN 978-1-594-9804-73

This book is dedicated to my six grandkids.

Contents

"Jesus Christ demands [an] unrestrained, adventurous spirit.... If a person is ever going to do anything worthwhile, there will be times when he must risk everything by his leap in the dark."

—Oswald Chambers, *My Utmost for His Highest*

Earliest Memories

I was born on Twelfth Street in Salem, Oregon, in the bedroom of my mother's childhood home. That's where she had all three of her boys, I understand. My family lived on a prune farm between Salem and Albany at that time, March 5, 1928, so I assume they took me back there after a few days.

We were probably poor, but I didn't know it. I remember we didn't have a water heater. Mom had to heat our bath water on the stove, which was enough of an ordeal that we didn't bathe but once a week, on Saturday night (whether we needed it or not). I'm not sure, but more than one of us may have bathed in the same water. With no indoor plumbing, we used an outhouse and got water via a pump on the back porch. We had a tall windmill that drew water to the porch from a deep well.

One of my early memories is when Dad bought us one bicycle. Since I was the youngest, I didn't get to ride it until one Saturday night when both of my brothers had to take baths; I spent the whole time trying to get on without success. Another memory is that we liked to play in the creek. We'd capture little fish in a pool, then dam it up and chase them with a stick. Mom and Dad knew that our boots leaked, so we were not supposed to go in the creek, but we did, and suffered for it.

I don't know how many acres of prune trees we had on the farm. During harvest, Mom sewed pads on the knees of our pants. Dad and his helpers shook the trees with long hooks until the ripe prunes fell to the ground, while we picked them up and put them in boxes to be taken to our dryer. I had to pick a certain amount of prunes before I could play. We had at least one cow, along with pigs, chickens, and a team of work horses. There was an old Ford Model-T in the back yard that didn't work anymore. I understand that Mom used to have to crank that thing to start it, and at least once it kicked back. I think she drove it to school in Turner where she taught for a while until we kids distracted her. We had a smokehouse where dad cured meat when we butchered. I had to churn cream until it turned into butter, then afterward we enjoyed the buttermilk. I remember once seeing my oldest brother, Lowell, lying quite still under a tree in the back yard—he had fallen out of the tree. I guess he wasn't badly hurt.

Dad's father had owned this farm, but he died of skin cancer before I came along, and Dad had to leave Pacific College (now George Fox University) to take over. He said there are only two things you must do: pay taxes and die. He first tried to get a job at a funeral home, but they told him he had too many noisy kids; he applied at the post office and got a job in Albany. He was a substitute carrier at first but was soon working steadily enough that we moved there in 1935 when I was eight years old.

Although we moved Dad off the farm, we couldn't get the farm out of Dad. We took along a cow, and I had to help milk her. We hadn't been in our new home long before we decided we needed to tear it down and build a new house. While we were doing that, we moved across the street into the barn. If I forgot to close a door and someone asked, "Were you born in a barn?"—I could say, "Almost." I got to help pound some nails in the new house. I remember feeling really good that I could let my new friend, Bob Govro, pound some nails.

I think it was while we were still living in the barn that we would swing on a rope from a limb of a tree across the street. We'd start at the top of the hill and swing out, dropping to the bottom of the hill—not very smart, huh? My older brother, Homer, dropped and broke his arm. Lowell once broke an arm while high jumping over a sawhorse in the yard. Of the three of us, I was by far the most rambunctious, but I've never had a broken bone. I broke a couple of teeth trying to pole vault over the barn fence. It was a bamboo pole with lots of spring, and when I came down, it bounced back up into my face and gave me a nice inverted V in my smile.

We used to spend a lot of time during the summer on the Willamette River. One time we found an old scow. We applied tar to the leaks and tried to paddle it across the river, but it would usually sink before we got across, and we would get out and push it the rest of the way. We had a neat sand bar on the other side. Mom thought I spent so much time in the water I might grow fins.

In Albany we attended a Methodist church. I don't remember hearing anything about how to be born again. The pastor didn't attend the prayer meeting, so my dad led it. When I was ten years old, I went to the daily vacation Bible school at the Evangelical church around the corner from our home, and when they gave an invitation to accept Jesus, I went forward. I asked Jesus to forgive my sins and come into my heart and to be my Lord and Savior. The next day I got my young friend to go forward. I never heard much about salvation after that until I got to college, and when I did, I had no sense that I needed to be saved again. My verse is Philippians 1:6: "Being confident of this very thing, that He who has begun a good work in you will complete it until the day of Jesus Christ." When I was a little older, I went over to that church one night when some men were giving testimonies. I was so moved I went into my parent's bedroom, weeping, when I got home.

In grade school I had a wonderful teacher, Mrs. Severson. She inspired me to begin writing poetry. She asked us to give a speech, I think in the fourth grade, and I preached a sermon on hell. These days I would probably be hauled into the principal's office and told I couldn't do that, but she didn't scold me. Rather she invited me to give that same sermon to her ladies group at church. Thus, my preaching career was launched. Maybe the real beginning was earlier.

Mom said when we were still on the farm, I used to line up fruit jars and preach to them. At least by the fifth grade I had enough of a sense that someday I wanted to be in ministry, that it motivated me to try to do well in my studies. I did well enough that my fifth-grade teacher advanced me to the seventh grade, although I think I lost some comprehension, especially of geography, by missing the sixth grade. I feel God made that up to me by letting me visit the countries in person, rather than just sitting and studying about them. My wife, Mary, said I've been to seventy-five countries in my career.

I don't remember much about my junior high days, except that some of us on the seventh-grade tumbling team became clowns and performed at the ninth-grade events. When I got to high school, I went out for track, and I wanted to pole vault. The coach had me run the half-mile every day to train. I got a job delivering special delivery letters for the post office. I wanted a motorcycle, but Dad resisted by bringing a motorcycle cop to our house to tell me that having a motorcycle would make three strikes against me from the start. But Dad did let me get a motorbike. Living about a mile from the post office, I would get up early to deliver letters before school, cranking up the motorbike and running alongside it to the post office as part of my training. I don't remember winning any races, except I won a stilt race once. They made fun of me and my homemade stilts before the race, but it turned out that I was the only one who could run on stilts. I did pretty well in pole vaulting. I jumped eleven feet two inches once, and that was with the old bamboo poles. In competition I think I was thirteenth in the state. I thought I was also pretty good at math to be able to figure that out.

I left home as soon as I graduated from high school. I went to work on a farm out of Harrisburg, Oregon, where I got to drive the tractors some. The son of the head man was an amazing driver. He could back two trailers with a loader behind them. I watched as he came to a gate, get off the cat while it was moving, open the gate and let the cat go through, close the gate and get back on. I tried it once, and the cat track really chewed up that gate. I was amazed that they were not harsh with me over that.

College

Because Dad had attended Pacific College (now George Fox University) in Newberg, Oregon, for one year, I decided to go there, too. My brother Lowell's wife was from Newberg and had attended Pacific. I started college in the fall of 1945. I hadn't played much basketball in high school, mostly church league ball, but in college I took it seriously. I was high point man in most games, maybe partly because the opposition expected me to shoot with my right hand, and I was left-handed. We had a student coach for a while, and I remember Harold "Spud" Ankeny and I were late for practice once, and he made us sit out a game. One time the story of our victory got into the Portland papers, and they spelled my name Nozard.

I played football, too. We didn't have enough players to field eleven, so we played eight-man football. I figured that our coach probably hadn't had a lot of winning seasons when one time during the half he came to me in awe and asked, "How does it feel to catch a touchdown pass?" We moved up to eleven-man football, but there was no platoon system in those days. Some of us were called sixty-minute men because we played the whole game. I was halfback and was often the only guy who could prevent a touchdown by the opponents. During one game when we were playing our rival school, Pacific University in Forest Grove, I hit one opponent so hard, my helmet came off; the next thing I knew we were in the next quarter. I had played a whole quarter out of my head. The first thing I was aware of was wondering how I looked to my girlfriend, Mary, who was in the stands. I went over to the coach and said, "Take me out, I can't remember the plays." He said, "Oh, you're doing fine," and left me in the game.

During the summer after my first year in college, I went back home and drove a dump truck for the county. I had to back the truck along a tarred line and spread gravel. I liked it. My coworkers knew I was planning to be a minister, and I felt the responsibility to live before them as a good example of a Christian. That summer I went to the Methodist youth camp at Barview on the Oregon coast and was strongly influenced by a guy named Dewey, a college student who was going to be a missionary. I was amazed at his grasp of Scripture and his strong emphasis on memorization. He inspired me to memorize 108 verses in the Navigator system that Dawson Trotman sponsored.

During that summer, Dad was appointed as lay preacher for the Methodist Church in Jefferson, about eight miles from home. I preached my first sermon there. I remember working very hard to prepare and then surprising myself and many of my listeners by being done in ten minutes.

Because I knew I wanted to be in ministry, I majored in Bible along with some speech and English literature classes—just maybe because Marv majored in English Literature, and I liked being near her. I entered the state After Dinner Speech Contest which was held on our campus. When one of our professors introduced me, he told a stupid joke—something about a guy whose tears ran down his back. I opened by saying, "It sounds to me like he had a bad case of bacteria," and I was off and running. I won that contest, though there were students competing from Oregon State and other big schools.

One day, Pop Knight, a part-time professor and dorm parent, invited everyone who was interested in singing in a male quartet to gather in a certain room and break into foursomes. When everyone had chosen their groups, there were four of us left whom nobody wanted, and we formed what became the Four Flats Quartet. The group members changed some as time went on, but I was part of the quartet from the beginning. We picked up two guys who had been in World War II; Ron Crecelius had a fabulous voice, and Dick Cadd was a little guy with a deep bass voice. We all had a pretty good sense of rhythm—Dick had been a drummer.

Chris (Crecelius) had come to college because he liked a girl who attended. He wasn't a Christian at first. We sang in many evangelistic services before he accepted Christ as his Lord—we had seen him cling to the pew in front of him 'til his knuckles turned white rather than respond to the invitation.

The Four Flats

The Four Flats and our wives.

I had prepared a list of reasons he should accept Christ, and during one of the spiritual life meetings, I asked him to turn it over and write a list of the reasons he should not accept Christ. He fumbled with the paper for a while, then said, "I guess there aren't any." That night when the invitation was given he was one of the first to go to the altar, and we prayed with him into the night. He became not just a Christian, but a very effective preacher.

In those spiritual life meetings, I learned that we all receive the Holy Spirit when we receive Christ, but there is a greater filling of the Holy Spirit, "purifying their hearts by faith" (Acts 15:9). I wanted that. I went out after one of those meetings, sat on the running board of a friend's car and prayed my heart out for the Holy Spirit to fill me. I felt like nothing happened.

Later the quartet was in meetings in Idaho, and Lowell Roberts, who later was president of Friends University in Wichita, Kansas, preached on the filling of the Holy Spirit, and I went to the altar. He knelt to pray with me. He said, "Norval, do you know anyone whom you think is filled with the Spirit?" I said, "Yes," thinking of him. Then he showed me that the Scripture says: "This is the will of God, your sanctification" (1 Thessalonians 4:3). And "If we ask anything according to His will, He hears us, whatever we ask, we know that we have the petitions that we have asked of Him" (1 John 5:14–15). He told me to completely yield my life to God and ask him for the filling with the Holy Spirit and believe that he answers that prayer. I did that, and I feel that he has walked with me through all my life.

Roy Clark, our choir director, encouraged us to go to the first Northwest Barbershop Harmony Contest in Forest Grove. He coached us to some pretty good barbershop singing (even filling in as baritone), and we got together some scroungy costumes. We won the contest and the prize of one hundred silver dollars. They took pictures of us afterward with the can-can girls, and when those photos came out in the Portland Oregonian the next day, it looked for all the world like Roy Clark had his arm around one of them. We went back the next year and won again. They eventually asked us not to come again because they were having trouble getting others to compete against us. Our wives formed a quartet and called themselves the Four Sharps, and they won second prize. As result of our victory, we were often asked to sing.

The quartet spent at least a couple of summers traveling together. On one trip across the country, we stayed in homes where we were served chicken dinner every night. We had a great time. Crecelius was a natural clown, and we did a lot of entertainment programs—especially for Christian kids at the end of the school year who didn't go to the prom. Although our program was designed for older kids, we once did a school assembly for grade school kids in Garibaldi, Oregon, near the coast. One of our routines said, "Do you know what they call potatoes in Idaho?" The answer is, "They don't call 'em, they dig 'em." But before we could get that answer out, the kids began to yell, "Spuds!" Later in a quiet pause during one of our songs, Chris said under his breath, "I'd like to wring their little necks." We cracked up and didn't make it through the rest of that song.

In my junior year I ran for student body president and our bass singer, Dick Cadd, ran for vice president. At the time we were helping to move buildings from Camp Adair (an abandoned World War II training facility) to campus, and before they put the final shingles on the roof of the library, Dick climbed up one night and wrote, "Hadley for President." Our wives and girlfriends campaigned for us, even singing a jingle to help us get elected—we won. Years later when they moved the building again, they found that sign on the roof.

We had lots of wonderful experiences. I used the quartet to announce my engagement to Mary, singing, "Mary Don't You Weep." I rewrote a verse, so it told that I had asked her to marry me, and since I sang those verses as a solo, at least two of the guys in the quartet didn't know what was coming.

When something special came to town, we were often asked to sing—and Bob Pierce was special. He had founded World Vision, and in those days was a prominent Youth for Christ speaker. When he came to the YFC rally at the Portland Civic Auditorium, we were on the program. Bob liked quartets, having once sung in one.

We sang at the annual YFC convention at Winona Lake, Indiana, when Bob returned from Korea after the outbreak of war. He told of pastors who were persecuted, some of them living in caves, and some living under the floor boards of their houses, being fed through the cracks by their wives—even their kids not knowing where they were. He said he knew the Koreans would love our music and invited us to return there with him. He said, "I can't promise you that we will get back home safely, but I can promise you that you will have a great ministry." After Billy Graham heard Bob speak about the needs in Korea, he said that although he was to have a new 1950 Bel Air Chevrolet delivered to him, he had canceled his order and was giving the money to help in Korea.

We knelt down on our knees in the Westminster Hotel and dedicated our old cars to the Lord, praying with our wives about how we should respond to Bob's invitation. It was a time of "willing to die" commitment to the Lord; we were willing. Because of the war, we were not able to obtain visas, so we couldn't go right then. (Bob was classified as a war correspondent, so he was able to stay with the Koreans throughout the conflict). We did go in 1955, however.

I need to go back to the end of December 1948. Mary and I had planned to be married after we graduated, but the quartet had such a busy schedule for that summer, we moved the date up to December 16, just before Christmas vacation. We got a letter from J. C. McCloud, a banker from Seattle, asking us to sing for a breakfast at one of their conventions on December 17. It was written on the stationery of a Portland hotel where he was staying. The guys said, "Oh no, Norv, we can't do that, not the morning after your wedding." But he had offered us more money than we had ever made from one engagement, and I knew that if I turned it down just because I was getting married, those three guys would lose their share of that money. I prayed about it for some time and finally drafted a reply, saying that we would be there. We were on our way to an engagement and I had the letter ready to mail, and Chris took it, and tore it up, saying, "No, Norv, we can't let you do this." It turns out there was no such guy as J. C. McCloud. The quartet guys had gotten the letterhead from the Portland hotel and written the fake invitation themselves.

After we were married, we had a flat tire on my little Ford coupe on the way to our motel. Even getting married during Christmas vacation didn't keep the quartet from playing a prank. We had an engagement at the Portland Country Club the night after our wedding. After we'd sung, Mary and I said goodbye to the quartet guys and went our way. They said goodbye but followed us. We stopped for ice cream in Milwaukie, and while they were sneaking around suspiciously near a bank, a police officer questioned them. When they'd followed us clear to our motel, they were prowling around, and Chris slipped on some ice and kind of hurt himself. They didn't have the nerve to disturb us, but they got a taxi driver to bring us a message, just so we'd know they were there.

We took our honeymoon by driving Dad's car to Sacramento. We liked California even then. I'd been there on a trip with my family, and once when I was about ten, a truck driver relative of Mom's, Orin Swain, had taken Homer and me to Los Angeles in his big eighteen-wheel truck; so we chose California for our honeymoon destination. We stopped one night in Yreka on the way and stayed in the worst motel of our lives—it even had bed bugs.

After the quartet won the barbershop harmony contest, we had lots of invitations to sing. Harlow Ankeny arranged our appointments, and I was the quartet treasurer. Then an agent in Portland named Norm decided he could make some money off us and offered to arrange for non-church engagements. He was good at getting us into conventions, radio and TV shows, and civic clubs. But soon he was booking us into nightclubs where there was a lot of drinking, and we didn't feel comfortable—we didn't want to compromise our Christian testimony or embarrass our Quaker college. We cautioned him a couple of times, but he didn't like it when we turned down opportunities. Once he became excited, saying Bob Hope and Bing Crosby were coming to do a show in the largest auditorium in Portland, and we were invited to be on the program. We got pretty excited about that, too, but then found that it was on a night when we were already booked in a Salem church. We told Norm about the conflict and he told us to cancel the church appointment, that this was an opportunity of a lifetime. We asked for some time and gathered to pray about what we should do. We knew when we got on our knees what was right. When we turned that one down, Norm quit scheduling us; it was a turning point in our quartet career. We had decided to put God ahead of fame or money.

The Four Flats 1950 from left to right:
Dick Cadd, Ron Crecelius, Norval Hadley,
Harlow Ankeny.

Alaska

The summer after Mary and I graduated, the quartet traveled for Youth for Christ and the National Association of Evangelicals. We were invited, along with our wives, to cruise to Alaska on the *Willis Shank*, a converted 125-foot minesweeper that had been made over into a missionary medical ship, skippered by Captain Stabbert. When we pulled into northern Canadian or Alaskan villages where they had no streets, just board sidewalks, I would ride my unicycle through town on those boardwalks. When I got back to the ship, a crowd of kids would be following me. We would then announce our meeting, and some told us that everyone in town, if they were not out fishing, would come. We sailed up to Juneau, stopping at several villages for meetings. We came back on the *Princess Louise*, a luxury liner. It was a great experience.

We traveled that whole next year, Randall Emry standing in for Harlow since Harlow had to finish college. We traveled the United States in two cars for a time because we had our families with us. The two couples with kids were in the lead car, a boy and a girl. I remember they stopped periodically and an arm with a blue potty would come out of the left side and an arm with a pink potty out of the right side, dump the waste and go on our way. It was an exciting evening in Kansas when Carolyn Cadd walked for the first time.

I figure that the first year of our marriage, I was away from home one-third of the time. I don't recommend that. Those were days when we were influenced by dynamic people like Bob Pierce to be willing to burn out for the Lord. I now know there must be a balance between commitment to ministry and being a good husband and father. One time after the quartet had been on the road a lot, I wrote a poem in which I said, "Absence as some sage had said does make the heart grow stronger. I'd rather take my wife along, and both grow fonder yonder."

Seminary

After our year in quartet ministry, I enrolled in Western Evangelical Seminary. That was1951. Mary and I were planning to go to Asbury Seminary in Kentucky, because a famous theology professor was there. But after we had packed all our stuff in a trailer and made it to Mary's folk's place in Idaho, we learned that he had left the seminary; we turned around and returned to Portland. One of the best things I got out of seminary was an appreciation for the power of prayer. I had taken a course in college on the history of revivals, and I wanted to be anywhere there was prayer for spiritual awakening. Some of us gathered at noon every Wednesday to pray; then it became every day at noon. We didn't see wide-spread, sweeping revival, but we began to notice that God was working in wonderful ways in each of our weekend ministries.

I sold Wilknit socks during seminary to help pay expenses. By selling at a certain level, I got a new Chevrolet, and as long as I kept up that level, Wilknit made the payments. I also served as assistant pastor at Salem Evangelical Church.

It was during those seminary days I began playing golf at the Oregon City golf course. David was born while I was in seminary, and I remember him welcoming me home from class almost with the same enthusiasm as our dog did in later years.

When I graduated in 1954, we had offers to pastor at an Evangelical, a Methodist, and a Friends church. In prayer, it seemed clear that we should accept the invitation to Forest Home Friends Church in Camas, Washington, moving from the Methodist to Friends membership. I pastored there for just over a year. That was when we first began to watch television. One of our members had a set, and we would go there and watch *I Love Lucy*.

First Asia Trip

Next, I was invited to pastor the Parkrose Friends Church on the east side of Portland, where I served for about one year. In the middle of that ministry, World Vision and Youth for Christ invited the quartet to make a nine-week tour of Asia. The night before we were to leave for Asia, we were booked in a Jack Shuler crusade meeting in Portland. He asked people to pray for our trip and to meet us in the back after the service if they would like to help us with the last $1,000 or so we needed. They provided the entire amount.

We traveled to Japan, Taiwan, Korea, Okinawa Island, Hong Kong, and the Philippines. We took Herschel Thornburg along with us. He could play piano and accordion and was a skilled artist who drew pictures while we sang. It was a great adventure and a very successful evangelistic ministry.

I wrote home on September 21 that we had been in seven meetings that day, and over five hundred came to Christ. One meeting was in a girls school where they treated us very enthusiastically. Then we went to a hospital where many wanted to hear us, but they didn't have an auditorium large enough, so we sang in a garage. One day the Youth for Christ director dragged us around to, I think, nine meetings. At the last meeting we were in a prison, and when we finished singing, the Youth for Christ director said to the inmates, "Don't you wish you had the joy, and the enthusiasm these fellows have?" He turned to gesture toward us sitting on the platform, and two of us were asleep! Rising to the challenge he said, "And the peace."

On September 10, we went from Tokyo to Seoul, Korea, to help at a World Vision pastors conference. We stayed for eight days, singing in schools during the day and at the conference at night. I wrote that 165 students signed decision cards in one school. There were thirty-three hundred pastors at the conference, planned by Bob Pierce to strengthen them after the trials they had been through in the war when North Korean forces targeted Christian leaders.

One night after Major Smith of the Salvation Army, London, spoke on the baptism with the Holy Spirit, at least twelve hundred stood to receive that blessing, and the church was full of praying Christians all that night. I was impressed by attending one of the 5:30 a.m. prayer meetings, which had been going on since the Korean War. Much of the prayer was for the unity of Korea—which still needs to be answered. We were never in a church service in Korea that was not packed out. One Sunday afternoon we had a meeting on South Hill, which was the largest Christian gathering in the history of that city. They took a picture from an airplane and estimated there were eighty thousand there. There was more praying than preaching.

On Monday, September 19, we flew back to Tokyo. We had meetings in schools and hospitals and factories during the day and in auditoriums at night. Once we went out of Tokyo just one hundred miles to a village of Numazu. The road was so bad it took us four hours. They told us there were only five hundred Christians in that village. We had a meeting for two nights in their largest auditorium. At least one thousand filled that hall, with many having to stand. They said it was the largest Christian gathering ever held in that town, and each night it seemed that about half of them stood, saying they wanted to accept Christ. We spoke through an interpreter and were not sure they understood what they were doing. We asked them to sit down and gave the invitation again, trying to be clear. We went back to the hotel and sang to the maids because they had wanted to come to our meeting but couldn't. Dale Cryderman, the Youth for Christ director, explained what we were doing and shared steps to conversion, and three women accepted Christ.

We sang outdoors at Shimbashi Station where one million people pass through every day. Thousands gathered just to watch us set up. We did two services, and 264 people signed decision cards. We sang at a seminary, in a meeting with forty-two missionaries, and in some meetings for the One Mission Society, formerly known as the Oriental Missionary Society. I preached in one of their churches on sin, and of the sixty in attendance, twenty came forward for prayer.

We went from Tokyo to Okinawa, and while there, we thought we were serenading the wife of one of the missionaries who was about to give birth in a kind of Quonset hut hospital. We found later we had been serenading the women's rest room. Dick tells some good stories about that trip in his book, *Four Flats and a Pitch Pipe*. There were sixty thousand Americans on Okinawa, and they had done a lot to make it an attractive tourist stop. We had fifty people in one service and sixty in another indicate a desire to receive Christ.

While we were in the Philippines, Dick got his call to return there as a missionary. Hundreds accepted Christ and asked for follow-up literature in those meetings. We offered a Bible study course to those who responded to our messages and were told we averaged one hundred responses a day. We had Jack Conner with us, who was skilled on the marimba and had played with the Xavier Cugat Band. We went to a military base outside of Manila, and Jack played with some very skilled Filipino musicians. I remember that music would just raise you out of your chair.

When we got ready to leave the Philippines for home, I could not find my passport. I had gone as far as we could in the airport without it, and had to let the other guys go on. There I was, outside, sweat pouring off my face, pawing again through my luggage while the others were about to board the plane. Then at the last moment Herschel pulled my passport out of his bag and said, "Look what I found." He had apparently held them for us in his bag while we were traveling so we wouldn't lose them. So I scrambled and made it onto the flight with the rest of our guys. We had been gone so long that when we got home, our children looked at us kind of funny—like they were thinking, "Who is this?"

With World Vision

After that adventure, Bob Pierce invited us to become the World Vision Quartet, just as they were moving from Portland to the Los Angeles area. We were asked to travel to Los Angeles and pick out homes early in 1956. Mary was pregnant with Marcia, and she had the mumps so bad she had to stay in the motel in Eagle Rock, the town World Vision was moving to, and could not go house hunting with us. After looking for most of a week, we found homes in Glendora; three of us on Lemon Street, and Chris two blocks away. I bought mine for $11,500. We did drag Mary out of the motel to see the house just before we left to go back to Portland. (Incidentally, Marcia has never had the mumps.)

We moved in the summer of 1956. That year World Vision sent us to sing for a week at the Billy Graham Crusade in Oklahoma City. It was a privilege to be with that team. We called them Christian royalty. We were impressed by the extent to which they were to avoid any appearance of wrongdoing. When we were traveling around in a car, Cliff Barrows would ask us to sing "Carolina in the Morning" (they were from North Carolina).

We became good friends, and Cliff and his new wife were still on our Christmas card list many years later.

We sang on the World Vision broadcast which was released over the ABC network on about 130 stations. World Vision hired Les Barnett, a converted Hollywood musician, to coach us and write arrangements for us and play for us. We also had Loren Whitney, a famous organist with the Haven of Rest programs, play for us. In fact, he owned the studio from which we made the broadcasts. We learned a lot of new songs for that ministry. Between recording sessions, we traveled the United States. We probably sang in most of the states, traveling mostly by car. We bought a stretch Cadillac—probably a former funeral car. We could stretch out and do our office work or sleep in the back. We knew people would criticize us for having such a fancy car, but we only paid $357 for it and felt we should put a sign in the window, "I'll bet we paid less for ours than you did for yours." I would preach one night, and Chris would preach the next—I think we complemented each other. I would have a lot of Scripture teaching in my messages, and he preached with a lot of emotion and passion; many came to Christ in our meetings.

We took another trip across the United States in July 1957. Mary and our three little kids stayed with her parents on the farm near Richfield, Idaho, while we traveled. I wrote to her on July 1 to describe a typical agenda—if anything, really, was typical: We passed a lot of towns, so it was hard to keep a 50-mile-per-hour average, but we arrived at our destination in Rockford, Illinois, by 6:00 p.m. even though Illinois was on daylight time and we lost another hour. We went to a hotel and changed and went to the Youth for Christ rally in the Rockford theatre building without any supper. The summer crowd was small, and over 75 percent were youth. A few raised hands for prayer, but no one came forward. They gave us $40 and bought about twenty records. . . . The Sunday morning service in the Free Church was good. We sang for Sunday school and then furnished music for the service, which was broadcast. Don Hoke of the Japanese Christian College in Tokyo was the speaker. We were with him in Tokyo. He wrote for *Christian Life Magazine*. They gave us $35. About six hundred were present. We ate at the Andersons' (our hosts), then slept, ate again and went to our evening service at an independent tabernacle. The crowd was small, about 180. We showed the World Vision film, and the offering was $129—praise God. The film really helped. I closed, and one raised a hand. We sang on their broadcast and then at 9:45 ate in their youth room, entertained some students, and got to bed at the Andersons' again by 11:30.

I found a flyer for a meeting in Murdo, South Dakota, probably on that same trip:

> Special tonight only!!! You are invited to hear The Visionaires quartet at 8:00 p.m. tonight, June 27, at the Murdo Auditorium. This quartet can currently be heard on the World Vision radio program which is broadcast over a nationwide network on

Sunday afternoons. They will be here in person tonight to present a unique blending of gospel songs, hymns, and spirituals and barbershop singing. If you like good music be sure and attend. You will enjoy this. No admission charge. A free will offering will be taken.

(We were known as the Visionaires for only a short time when we first joined World Vision, and soon took the name the World Vision Quartet.) The interesting thing is that in February 2014, I was invited to speak at the sixtieth anniversary of Revival Prayer Fellowship in Bismarck, North Dakota, and Bob Thune, the pastor of a large Evangelical Free Church, came up to me and said, "Are you Norval Hadley?" I said, "Yes." He said, "Were you in the Four Flats Quartet?" I said, "Yes." He said, "You came and sang at my church in Murdo, South Dakota, when I was just a kid."

We went on to Winona Lake, Indiana, on that trip to the Youth for Christ International Convention, and I wrote home about meetings with Frank Phillips and Bob Pierce (our bosses), and Merv Rosell (the evangelist). Bob preached his heart out, and hundreds came to salvation and to dedicate their lives to the Lord. Dr. Phillips had just come from Korea and said they wanted the quartet for a month in Japan, and he wished someone would underwrite that trip. Bob Pierce said he felt he should someday go to Australia, and he would like us to go with him—but neither of those trips materialized. It was hard to think of having to be away from family for a long time again. We were on the program with some wonderful people like Marj Saint whose husband, Nate, was a pilot and one of the five missionaries killed in Ecuador; Bill Carle, a famous soloist; Dr. Bob Jones; and Dr Clyde Narramore. Dr. Roy McKewon, Youth for Christ leader from Los Angeles, introduced us as the greatest quartet in America. He said the chef at the Beverly Hilton Hotel had told him he'd seen all the groups who performed there but never saw entertainment better than our quartet.

From Winona Lake, we went on to New York City where we enjoyed the Billy Graham Crusade meetings and did some recording. The Graham team greeted us warmly, especially Cliff Barrows, and gave us tickets for special seats. It was the biggest crowd ever in the Madison Square Garden, and hundreds came forward—one in fifteen. Lila Trotman, wife of Dawson Trotman, the recently drowned founder of The Navigators, spent a half hour with us in the hotel lobby. She said the night before Dawson died, the Lord showed her he was going to die; when she told him, he spent hours giving her instructions for how to carry on the Navigators ministry for the next ten years. We traveled through Washington DC to Salem, Ohio, then met Roy Clark in Emporia, Kansas. After ministering in Denver with pastor Lloyd Hinshaw, we arrived back to our wives and families.

I found mail indicating that in October of 1957, the quartet was in Medford, Oregon, for meetings in the Friends church there. Marilyn would have been less than three and Marcia about one year old. I marvel at all Mary had to cope with while we were away from home. She was teaching a Sunday school class, hosting a Tupperware party, buying dishes and other things for the children and the household, as well as coping with the children's health problems.

Later in October, we had meetings in Vancouver, British Columbia, and we sang also in some large churches. In one Youth for Christ rally there were five hundred present. Several were saved in those meetings. We stayed with the McPherson family, and they took us in like we were their children, which resulted in a long-term relationship. We went from there to Tacoma, where in one rally there were seven hundred in attendance, then to Yakima, Washington, for Youth for Christ meetings and ministry in churches. I wrote home about Youth for Christ taking us to an up-scale restaurant where the meals cost $2.50, and to a hotel where we had to pay $4 for rooms. We had up to five school assembly meetings a day, plus maybe a breakfast meeting and a church meeting at night. I wrote home about meetings when up to fifteen responded to our invitation to accept Christ, even on nights when I felt I preached with little unction.

In January 1957, when we had been with World Vision just over a year, Bob Pierce invited us to help in an evangelistic crusade in the Philippines, our second trip to Asia as a quartet. As part of the crusade, we sang during the day in schools, businesses, and prisons. Les Barnett, a gifted pianist and arranger, was with us. He had been saved while he was working in Hollywood. We knew that Les was not sober when we were in Hawaii on the way over—he said pineapple affected him that way. When we were praying before a meeting in the Sunken Gardens, Bob prayed, "Lord, if I get in your way, just remove me, and I pray that for all my team members." Later we were singing at a school, and one of the boys had a really nice-looking motor scooter. Les asked if he could ride it, and he went down the road just about a block, lost control, and crashed it into a ditch. He had to go to the hospital with a broken rib that had punctured his lung. We couldn't help but think of Bob Pierce's prayer. A few months later Les died of that injury.

We had three weeks of meetings in the open air, and some nights it rained. In that climate, people were in danger of getting sick when they got wet, but still large numbers came to the meetings, and many came forward to receive Christ as Lord. One night it was estimated there were ten to twelve thousand people who attended, and 229 made a decision to follow Christ. Another night there were 393 who responded to the invitation, and at another 491. That night I counseled with the son of a United Church missionary. A writer for a large magazine gave his heart to the Lord. After the service a large group of missionaries came to our hotel and expressed their appreciation for our ministry. Toward the end of the meetings I wrote home that 3,321 had made decisions during the meetings.

We were invited one day to the home of Mr. Go, a wealthy Chinese businessman. He had a beautiful swimming pool, and I got comfortable diving from a high platform. I learned to do flips and a gainer. We even enjoyed his bowling alley. We were invited to the palace for a meeting with President Magsaysay. We were supposed to have twenty minutes, but he enjoyed our music and Bob's prayer for him, and we stayed for over an hour. He said, "Gosh, you guys can sure sing." We were able to share with him the plan of salvation. About a month later he was killed in a plane crash. We hope to see him in heaven. We stayed in a nice hotel near the Sunken Gardens. At first the food was great, but I remember as the days wore on, everything began to taste like fish.

After the trip to Asia we traveled a lot in the United States for World Vision. I found an itinerary beginning May 5, 1958. We went to Citrus Heights, California; to Brookings, Salem, and Portland, Oregon; then Seattle, Yakima, Wenatchee, Spokane, Richland (where Dick Cadd's brother Bob lived), and Walla Walla, Washington; and finally to Twin Falls and the Boise area in Idaho. We arrived home on May 21. We were often in Youth for Christ meetings, selling records and offered to help people sign up to sponsor children through World Vison. I would preach one night and Chris the next. There were many conversions and other commitments to Christ.

In August of that year, we drove to Billings, Montana. Two hundred came to our meeting, we sold thirty-seven records, and three took orphan sponsorships. The offering was $177, which was better than in most meetings. We went into Alberta,

Canada, on some muddy dirt roads. I wrote home on that trip that I wondered if God wanted Mary and me to become missionaries—I knew Dick had committed to missionary ministry. I wanted to serve so I would not always be away from family. We drove through the beautiful Canadian resort Lake Louise on that trip. While we were away, Mary took our three children to be with her parents on the farm near Richland, Idaho. Marilyn was injured while there and had to have several stitches.

In October 1958, we had a series of meetings in a church in Turlock, California. We sang in a school assembly, and two teachers said it was the best assembly program they ever had. The kids were usually so disorderly they had thought of not having more assemblies, but we held their attention. We helped to improve the relationship between the Youth for Christ director and the principal of that school. A host took us water skiing, and I learned to ski on one ski.

In April 1959, we were invited to a quartet festival at Barclay College in Haviland, Kansas. We went on the train, and when we got off, our luggage didn't. We were dressed in scrubby clothes. We chased the train to the next town, but no luck. Roy Clark, our musical father and now professor at Barclay, took us to Penney's department store in Pratt, and amazingly they had four suits alike that just fit us. I got the only size 41 they had in the store. The suits were on sale for $35 each, and with shirts and ties it came to $192. Roy told our sad story in the meeting that night, and they gave us $172 in a special offering. They had the largest crowd ever gathered in Haviland, and they bought all the records we had with us. Our suitcases had gone on to another city, but we eventually got them back.

In late October 1959, we hauled a trailer behind Dick's Packard through Albuquerque to Booker, Texas, and on to Tulsa, Oklahoma. I wrote from Tulsa that we had visited the office building of the television evangelist Oral Roberts. I wrote, "It's a heaven on earth built around their god, Oral Roberts." I wanted to know, amid all the luxury, what they were doing for missions, and when we got to their literature department I found out without asking. They were printing and distributing literature in about a hundred different languages, all promoting Oral Roberts. We saw his throne room. He had a phone with about two dozen buttons, so he could control his kingdom. They had a fifteen-hundred-seat auditorium. Our host took us to a restaurant, and then to our service in an American Baptist Church. There were about 225 there. They gave us $100, and ten people raised hands in commitment after my message on "The Value of a Soul." We went on to Indianapolis where we attended a Billy Graham meeting. We came back through Rockford, Illinois, Wichita, and Oskaloosa, Iowa, where we had a meeting at William Penn College.

On November 4, we were at Malone College in Canton, Ohio. In a chapel service, I closed with a testimony of the quartet and twenty-five students raised hands, asking for prayer that they might yield their lives to the Lord. The dean and the speech professor said they had been there twenty years and they enjoyed our visit more than any they could remember. Before the offering at an evening service, Howard Moore, whom we had visited in Taiwan where he was a missionary, said that his two children had made their first step spiritually when we were with them in Taiwan. Chris spoke, and seven came forward, some weeping. One quit a two-year battle against a call to be a missionary.

We'd had so much trouble with the Packard that we sold it for $150 and picked up a new '59 Pontiac to drive West for the dealer. We had to put a trailer hitch on it and had a little trouble when we found that it didn't have any anti-freeze, but no harm was done.

I wrote home in January 1960 after we had sung at the Hollywood Women's Club on our way to Medford. We were at a tea hosted by Mae Norton afterward, and she could hardly get a word in because ladies were complimenting us on our program. We got a motel at Williams, California, at 2:30 a.m. and had to use chains over icy roads in the Mt. Shasta area. We got to the home of Clynton Crisman, the Friends church pastor in Medford, by 5:15 p.m. I preached at a school assembly the next day and at a church meeting, and there was a good response. An eighteen-year-old woman sought help. We made that trip in our Cadillac limousine. It was nice—Harlow could set up his office in the back seat, and I could stretch out and sleep. They let me drive a lot because they said I was the only one who could sleep while I was driving! We had meetings in

Medford at the Friends church, in schools, and on the lone TV station; followed by meetings in Talent where they increased attendance dramatically; then at Ashland Friends Church. There were many who came to the altar for victory, up to seven a night.

In 1960, World Vision sent us to New York City to help introduce their new representative, Dick Hamilton, to the churches. We stayed in the Salisbury Hotel, owned by Calvary Church. On the way from the airport to the hotel in a cab we started to practice, and the cab driver turned the radio on. I asked him to turn it off, and we sang one we knew he would enjoy. Only in New York.

We held meetings in a different church each night, but our day times were free. Our hotel was right in the theatre district, so I went to a show at the Music Hall with about ten thousand other people—we thought with their accent the people all sounded like comedians. I got a real fast haircut for sixty cents. It was cold, fifteen degrees with snow on the ground.

We learned that there were TV shows being filmed nearby during the day time and decided we would try to get on some shows. I remember that I got on *Concentration*. I was given clues and was supposed to guess what city was being spelled out. It was Scranton, Pennsylvania, but I was such a westerner I didn't know about Scranton. I got a consolation prize, which was a Polaroid camera. While we were waiting to see if I would get on *Concentration*, we took a boat out to the Statue of Liberty, and I walked the narrow circular stairway to the crown. Dick got on *The Price is Right*, and he had done enough shopping with his wife that he won and got a lot of silver. He had to pay $130 excise tax and $260 income tax. We kept some of the silver settings in our home while the Cadds were overseas.

I went to watch *The Perry Como Show* taping. Perry was wearing a red sweater, and the producer said it would not work. Mary had just given me a beautiful new blue sweater for my birthday, and I motioned an usher over and offered my sweater—and they used it. I was so excited I called home and said, "My sweater is going to be on TV!" Perry said they should recognize me in the credits.

In November of that year we conducted a week of meetings at Booker Friends Church in Texas. It was an interesting week. We went shooting a couple of times with borrowed guns. Chris would preach one night and I the next. I had some compliments on my preaching that were so nice I had to share them in a letter with my wife. The pastor said people had been saying that I could step right into any college or university church and really fill the bill. His wife said she felt I should be in a Bible school or somewhere because I made things clear. One man said, "If I could preach that good I would be a preacher too. You make it look so easy." A friend we knew from college brought a group of young people from over sixty miles away one night, and it just happened that my message was just right for young people. A couple of young women found the Lord. I preached on sanctification in one of our last sessions. I thought it was a very common message and not so good, but twelve to fifteen people came forward. Afterward one said I would do the Friends church a disservice if I didn't have that message published. The Saturday night meeting lasted until after 10:00 p.m. because so many wanted to give testimony. I described it in a letter as near revival. One said she hated to see us leave more than any other visitors that had come to Booker.

On November 29, 1960, we went to Barclay College in Haviland, Kansas, where they were having a pastors gathering, and again the Lord used us and several came to the altar. After Chris spoke in one service, thirty-four people came to the altar. I told him I thought he was at the apex of his career. We sold $130 worth of records. Roy Clark was teaching at Barclay, and if I remember correctly, had eight children in his family then—mostly girls. He was famous for his reading of the poem, "The Touch of the Master's Hand." We mimicked him in an entertainment program saying, "It was battered and scarred but the auctioneer thought he'd just give it a whirl—*Sorry folks, I've got to go home, we just had another girl.*"

While we were on that trip toward the end of 1960, we knew that World Vision was about to release us as a quartet. We were all thinking and praying about what to do next. We had been invited to work in the World Vision office, and I was thinking seriously about that, while Dick and Helen Cadd had decided to be missionaries in the Philippines. I received an invitation to mission work in Africa, and in my letters home, Mary and I were thinking that through, but I was leaning toward the World Vision job. I could serve the whole world from there.

I was asked to head the correspondence department at World Vision, and I did so for a year. I answered letters written to the president, Bob Pierce. He liked my work and after a year invited me to come into his office as his assistant. In offering me the job, they said I would be Bob Pierce's alter ego—the other Bob Pierce. I needed to be comfortable with anonymity, because I would do things in the name of Bob Pierce, and he would get the credit. He was the kind of leader who, if he had two or three good people around him, could accomplish two or three times as much. We worked together very well. I would store up his incoming mail while he was away, then often go to his home when he returned and in an hour or two get through a week's correspondence. He would consider a letter and just say yes, or no, or dictate a few lines, and I would construct an answer from his words and send it over his signature.

In April 1961, Heini German-Edy, Swiss missionary to Indonesia, came to the United States and I traveled with him for a couple of months. We spent some time in the San Francisco Bay Area where we had some effective services and viewed a 420-ton shipment of goods going out from the Naval Supply Center to Heini's work in Indonesia. I drove my brother Lowell's car from Portland to Albany where we visited my parents and had a meeting and an interview with the newspaper. Our meeting was taped by TV station KWIL. The next day, we rushed back to the Portland airport where Lowell and Mona met us. We got there at 10:30 a.m. for a 10:45 flight. They held the plane for fifteen minutes while a confused ticket agent processed us. We got to Spokane at 12:30, went to a motel and got some rest, then flew the next morning to Missoula, Montana, and on to Helena where it was snowing lightly. We went from there to Rockford, Illinois, where we had a meeting in a large church. The pastor explained that church leaders would not allow them to take an offering for us, but they would give a $25 honorarium. Then after Heini poured his heart out, they gave us $210. We then spent some time with World Vision representative Jim Franks in Grand Haven, Michigan, doing meetings and TV broadcasts in Muskegon. I sang a solo on one of the broadcasts. Then we went on to Chicago where there was seven inches of snow. It was a great experience for me to have that time with Heini and get his perspective on American excesses.

In December 1963, I went with Bob Pierce to Asia—first to Japan and then to Taiwan. I had a letter from Mary that described pretty well her life in my absence: "I've been busy since you've been gone, and my schedule looks even more hectic in the days ahead. [On the way home from seeing me off at the airport] I stopped at the bank and we looked around Nash's, got home around 10:30 or so. I was really tired, but cleaned and straightened the house somewhat, washed sheets, etc. and fell into bed."

On our way to Tokyo, we had to stop for refueling in Wake because of strong headwinds, and as a result we didn't get in until 6:00 p.m. instead of 4:45 as planned. Dr. Pierce took us to a very special Japanese restaurant, then we went to bed—we had been up about twenty-four hours. Missionary Bill Hulet took us on a tour of Tokyo, where I learned some interesting things. Many kinds of sin were practiced openly there. There was very little relationship between sex and what we think of as sin. For instance, a high school survey showed that most of the boys had a goal to become the patron of a geisha girl by age thirty-five.

On another trip with Larry Ward, probably in October 1964, we arrived in Seoul. Some precious children from the Korean Children's Choir who had traveled in the United States met us at the airport and pinned flowers on us. We went to Dr. Han Kyung Chik's Young Nak Presbyterian Church. Over ten thousand attended. We had lunch there with Dr. Frank Laubach (eighty-three years old). I was able to help Larry and local staff work through problems and decisions, because I had a great deal of background on projects. We went on to Hong Kong, to Saigon, and Indonesia. I wrote again on October 18 on our way from Bangkok to Saigon. We had stayed in the fascinating Ambassador Hotel in Hong Kong just overnight where I bought Mary a Swiss automatic, shock proof, twenty-four-jewel watch for $17.50.

In Bangkok, Larry wanted to take me to a special jewelry store he knew about. He called, and they sent a cab for us at their expense. We went way back into narrow alleys, then a boy led us past homes and shops, where no one could have found us if they didn't have a guide, to one of the most exclusive jewelry shops. The proprietress (who greeted Larry like a long-lost friend) was jeweler to the king. It was then I realized what a privilege it was to be traveling in Asia with Larry.

The landing in Saigon was memorable. The plane remained at a high altitude until we were almost there, then dove down to the runway to avoid gunfire. In Saigon I was to learn about our work, so I could make fund-raising calls to large donors and corporations. We went through the Cong Hoa Vietnamese Hospital for an hour and a half. It was not easy. They had about two thousand patients and were getting about sixty per day because of the fighting nearby. We were scheduled to take a plane at the air base from Can Tho to Da Nang, but it was late, and we figured we would not be able to make it there and back in time. We canceled that trip after we learned that Typhoon Clara was heading right to where we would have been. They expected twenty-four inches of rain, so we thanked the Lord for his protection. We took an army bus back into town and had a planning session with Dr. Pierce that night in his room at the Caravelle Hotel. After the meeting, we went up to the roof to watch and listen to the sounds of war. There was a cleared corridor in one direction where one could travel for eighteen to twenty miles safely but couldn't go three miles in other directions at night without trouble. There was a curfew for Americans, and we were not allowed on the streets from Saturday night until Monday morning because of an election, but there were no incidents. It was probably that Monday that Doug and I had a good meeting with fifty-five chaplains from all over Viet Nam.

I wrote home in November 1964 during a trip to Medford where I preached for about a week. I stayed in the home of the Evans family who said they were saved in meetings with our quartet in 1948. I rode a borrowed unicycle in youth meetings and gave object lessons. In one meeting six youth raised their hands wanting to be saved. We had some question and answer sessions because they said my preaching made them want to ask questions.

In late November 1964, World Vision sent me to South America to set up pastors conferences and to buy a truck in Brazil for relief work. I stopped in La Paz where the airport is at thirteen thousand feet; I was dizzy the whole time I was there. I went on to Medellín, Columbia, and Lucy Anderson met me at the airport. She was the sister of Roy Clark, and she and her husband Alvin served in the United States Information Service. I went on to Cochabamba, where we planned to hold the conference and met my contact Pete Wagner, a missionary with Bolivian Indian Mission. We made a presentation the next day to forty pastors and twenty missionaries who had gathered to plan an Evangelism in Depth conference. We were able to gather a committee and visit some possible sites for the conference.

Afterward, Pete urged me to take a bus ride to Santa Cruz with Harold Harrison, a missionary with World Gospel Mission who was returning from the planning meeting. It was a three-hundred-mile trip, through some moon-like country. Harold knew I had to go to Rio, and told me there were flights east from Santa Cruz, of which my travel agent was unaware. So I took a flight from there. We flew over jungle so thick that from the air it looked like a golf course. I had left my suitcase in Cochabamba and was traveling light, so we radioed Cochabamba and had them send my suitcase on to Lima, Peru, my next stop. I went from Santa Cruz, Bolivia, direct to Rio, Brazil, then on to Recife, where I bought a truck for use in relief work. The change in flights enabled me to go on back to Medellin and have more time in Guatemala to be with Friends missionaries and still get home by December 15. I wrote home that it was quite an experience to travel alone without proper currency, where no one spoke English. I had learned a lot from Peter Wagner, a great teacher, which helped me with the rest of my job on that trip. After flying from Medellin to Lima, I wrote home on December 5, 1964. When I tried to claim my suitcase, which had been sent from Bolivia, the office that should have had it was closed. They kept telling me, "Mañana." The next day I took the bull by the horns and took a bus to the airport. First no one had it. An airline worker found it with some papers on it, and for two hours we went from one official to another, got at least fifteen stamps and signatures, then had to do most of it over again because somebody got two numbers turned around. Noon was normally quitting time, but I wouldn't let them. At 12:30, after they told me for a half hour it was impossible, I finally got it. My contact, Dr. Money, said I was very fortunate. They had warned me about theft; there were three shirts missing along with five rolls of new film.

Dr. Money was from New Zealand and worked with Wycliffe. He took me out to a government-owned resort where we were to have the conference, and after meeting with a group of church leaders. I finished my time in Lima with the confidence that we would have a good conference. Although the leaders were all very busy in their own ministries, there was enough interest that they were willing to commit to it. Lima is often cloudy, but gets less than an inch of rain per year.

It was on that trip that I heard it said, "Our church is like a sack with two mouths—as fast as they come in at the top, they go out at the bottom," and, "Our church is like a prairie fire. It flares up then dies down again." I began to understand that although we may have been doing a good job of taking the gospel to every person, perhaps we were falling short in obeying the second part of the Great Commission, to "teach them all things that I have commanded." I searched and could not find a good book on the commands of Christ, so I started to write one. But my life was so full of responsibilities that I didn't finish it until forty years later when the National Prayer Committee helped me publish my fourth book, which is titled *Encountering Jesus*, co-authored by Kim Butts and Dave Butts.

At about this time I got a message asking if I would interview for an administrative position at George Fox College. I wrote home that considering my commitment to the mission and ministry of World Vision, I felt all right about turning down the invitation.

I found some letters I had written home in January 1966 while on a trip for World Vision into my old stomping grounds in Oregon and Washington. It began with a meeting in Ray Stedman's Peninsula Bible Church in Palo Alto, California, with sixty-five people there to view a World Vision film. I drove through up to four feet of snow past Mt. Shasta to my next stop in Newberg. The superintendent of Northwest Yearly Meeting asked me about coming to be his assistant; again, I did not feel released from World Vison. I showed the World Vision film in Salem and Lebanon and stayed with my brother Lowell in Portland. When I spoke at my seminary, Western Evangelical Seminary, they invited me back to be their speaker for Christian life week in May. I had a phone call with my boss, Bob Pierce, who had some projects he wanted me to help him with back home. He urged me to get pastors together in Portland and Seattle to see the film, and I managed to do that over a short period of time. He made me feel needed. I was asked to speak at the Seattle Memorial Friends Church. I wrote home that I had never before realized that people thought so much of me as a special speaker. I showed the film at the Tacoma Immanuel Baptist Church, and gave an invitation after the showing; a student wept as he accepted Christ. Then I drove back down to Newberg where I spoke at a George Fox College chapel service. I stayed and talked with some students after chapel, one of whom had lost his leg in an accident and blamed God. I led him to Christ, and he wondered if perhaps he could do something to help other amputees. I played golf with Harlow Ankeny. I then had film showings in the Albany Evangelical Church (where I was saved at the age of ten). There were 250 people there, and the offering was $250. After showings in Medford and Redding, California, I got a letter from home saying I was invited to speak at Quaker Gardens on February 25.

The next letter I found, I was writing home on October 10, 1967, while flying to Can Tho, Viet Nam, on a C-47, which is a twin-engine plane like a DC-3. It had canvas bench-type seats down each side, no rugs, no pillows, no coffee, and no flight attendant; but it was free transportation because I was employed by a volunteer agency, and this was Air America. I was the only one from World Vision on this trip. Larry Ward had gone to Seoul to get some projects started on our hospital grounds there, and Dr. Pierce went to Tokyo to be with Billy Graham. Mike, a Seabee from Port Hueneme, California, was sitting beside me in fatigues holding a rifle. He built clinics for public health, sometimes having to build during the day and fight at night. As we were taxiing out, we passed a big C-123 cargo plane that had been hit the night before by an F-125 while both were landing in the rain. Someone in the tower may have fallen asleep. The pilot of the jet was killed and four crew members of the C-123 were injured; both planes were wrecked. I was to meet Dick Pendell in Can Tho but could not reach him by phone when we got there because of a new dial system. A CORDS (Office of Civil Operations and Rural Support) driver took me to the area where he lived, and he found Dick using a map Doug Cozart had drawn for me. Dick was feeding twelve G.I.s and construction workers. I spoke to them about World Vision until about 10:45 p.m. and then tried to sleep next door to a Signal Corps barracks where they had music, movies, and parties every night. The next morning, we went to CORDS to arrange for a helicopter flight the next day to Vinh Binh to visit refugee work. We then went to the air base and talked to people who helped us. We ate in the officers club, and Dick took me to a school we supported and to visit the head of refugee work in CORDS. I took the Pendells out to dinner. Because they had no running water, we washed and showered in rain water which flowed off the roof. They had a new house near a police station that kept getting hit, so they were not allowed to move into it.

I wrote that I'd learned a lot of things. Some thought we should use A-bombs to end the war. President Thieu and one other candidate were the only ones who had ballots in the election in Can Tho. It was a dirty, complicated world.

I wrote again on October 10 that we'd had quite a day. We caught a chopper from Air America at 7:00 a.m. and flew to Vinh Binh province. I asked the pilots if anyone had ever shot at them. They said, "Oh yeah, there's a guy who sits at the end of the runway and shoots at everything that takes off all day long." I said, "Good night, can't you get him?" They said, "We don't want to—he hasn't hit anyone yet." We put down on a small strip and waited thirty minutes for an agriculture man we were to pick up, who apparently hadn't received our radio message. When he finally came, we took him and two United Nations counterparts and set out for Ben Cat, the new refugee village where a G.I. who had been in our film footage was shot by a sniper the morning after our crew filmed him. On the way, Dick made the decision not to go to Ben Cat because he figured if the ag man hadn't received our message, the patrol that was to protect us probably hadn't either. God led him. We landed at Tieu Can, about four kilometers away from where the patrol was based and were met by the district chief. The patrol was on an operation and had seen activity the night before. They got to bed at 11:00 p.m. and were up at 2:45 a.m. walking through Viet Cong territory, trying to flush out the enemy (we listened to the whole thing on a two-way radio). About 10:30, the patrol came in, muddy and weary but in good spirits. There were eight-five of them on the operation, but they had failed to control the Viet Cong. We asked the province chief if we should drive to Ben Cat now that we had protection, and he said to come back in a week or ten days. They were expecting more activity as they neared the October 31 date when they would celebrate the overthrow of Diem.

Our chopper came back for us on schedule, and we flew to Phu Vinh, seeing three Viet Cong road blocks on the way. We dropped off the ag man and got some food, which we took back to the guys we had just left because they were getting low. As we were circling over a river for landing, someone shot at us. When we landed, a major in charge met us, told us there had been some action out toward Ben Cat, and asked us to take them out to see where it was coming from. I thought, "Good night, can't they get their own helicopter?" But they got in with us, and we took them out. We flew at thirty-five hundred feet and only came down when over secure villages. Small arms fire was not much good above twenty-five hundred feet. On the road just before Ben Cat, right where we would have been traveling, was a big mine crater and trucks backed up a long way.

We went back to Tieu Can and were met by a sergeant who told us that six had been killed and three wounded and asked if we could wait thirty minutes or so to take in the wounded—which we did. Four wooden boats called sampans, full of Viet Cong, were on the river about one thousand feet from the road. They had triggered a mine as a group of entertainers went over it. The wife of one of the wounded rode back with us. She had been in a car in front of the one that was hit. The sampans came right into town, so we radioed for air support. In minutes, a single engine plane flew overhead with four rockets under each wing and shot them into the sampans, taking them out. Only two of the three we took back were seriously wounded. The comedian whose wife rode with us had a broken back that we roughly splinted. A Vietnamese man had a bad head and face wound and was wounded also in the hand and leg. A Jeep ambulance was waiting for us when we landed at Can Tho, while other choppers came in with more wounded as we waited for a flight back to Saigon. That patrol had recorded ten incidents in the preceding month, and this was the eighth one so far in October. They had "pacified" two hamlets of fifty in that district, one of which was Ben Cat—which wasn't very pacific that day! They planned for three the next year, making five of fifty in two years. It was going to be a long war.

Even when we got back to Saigon, things were tense. There was a sudden curfew, and employees were all gone. I tried to get USAID to come take us home and was told there would be no USAID bus, but nevertheless a bus came and took us. The streets were blocked by a parade. We stood behind Vietnam's only four-star general, General Vien, chief of defense. We saw President Thieu get into his glass-bubble Cadillac with about twenty motorcycle escorts. It was an exciting day in Vietnam.

I served as assistant to Dr. Pierce as long as he was president. When he left I was made director of World Vision relief organization. In April 1969, I was sent to Africa to start a relief program to help Christians in Biafra. The Ibo tribespeople had been blockaded and were starving, so relief agencies came to their rescue with relief flights. There were flights operated by the World Council of Churches and another operation run by the Red Cross, but evangelical Christians did not yet have a relief effort. I went through Copenhagen to Monrovia, Liberia. I'd stopped in Tunis and Dusseldorf but was not allowed to leave the plane on those stops. I had a letter from the Mayor of Monrovia, California, for the Mayor of Monrovia, Liberia. I made friends with a black man on the flight and asked him how I could meet an official. He said the best way is to be introduced by a higher official, then said he would arrange for me to meet the mayor. He turned out to be Robert Bright Sr., a member of Liberia's house of representatives. When we landed, he ushered me through and I got VIP treatment. He took me to the hotel in his fine Caprice. Monrovia was hosting a six-day conference of the Organization for African Unity, which attempted to resolve the conflict between the central government of Nigeria and the Ibo tribespeople of Biafra. I had lunch with some of the dignitaries from several nations. Mr. Bright arranged for the mayor to pick me up the next night and take me to a reception at his country club with the delegates to that conference. Emperor of Ethiopia, Haile Selassie, in his speech said both sides in the Nigerian crisis were on the verge of exhaustion and might be willing to make concessions. The mayor arranged for me to meet with the head of the Biafra delegation, the chief justice of their supreme court. I asked him what he felt could bring an end to the conflict.

On my flight from there to Cotonou (located on the coast of Benin, next to the country of Nigeria), I rode with a reporter from the *New York Times* and one from the *London Times*. Both said the conference in Monrovia was a fiasco—each side had been sent with instructions not to bend. The Biafra delegation walked out on the third day.

Cotonou had about one hundred thousand people, and was very French, but the economy was weak. Many slept on dirt or on boards, and very few had work. I met reporters who had failed to get clearance to enter Biafra. There were flights going into Biafra from Cotonou, and Red Cross flights going in from the island of São Tomé. Russ O'Quinn, a Christian pilot friend of World Vision, was in charge of the Red Cross flights. I wrote that it was perhaps the largest humanitarian effort in history. The Christian effort had hardly started, yet non-Christian agencies, even non-Americans, were giving tremendously. I was advised not to stay in Biafra very long, to take my own food and water, and to know that transportation and housing would be a problem.

My life was not dull. That Thursday, April 24, I wrote home that I was staying in a hotel with cottages in a courtyard. "Last night I had trouble sleeping. I must have been awake till 1:00 or 2:00 a.m. At 3:30 shouts at my door awakened me. I had been robbed of my billfold—which was on a stand right by my head—my date book, a check, some cash, my tape recorder, and mosquito netting. Guards saw, chased, and with the help of police caught the thieves. I went to the police station in the night and identified my belongings, then went back and followed the trail of the thieves and found my date book minus some notes, and the billfold minus $45. The thieves had wadded up every paper including $20 bills and thrown them down while they were being chased. All morning I've been at the police station signing papers." The thieves had a knife and a gun and would be sentenced to twenty years in prison. If I had just stirred, they might have killed me.

After getting some sleep, I went into town to get a suitcase to replace the one the airline had demolished. Then I checked out, arriving at the airport just in time to board the first Red Cross plane leaving with a load of supplies for the enclave. It was a big C-97 loaded with thirteen tons of soap. I was interested to learn that one of the essential things they carried was salt. We landed after two hours, having been given landing lights just for thirty seconds before we touched down. They used the C-97 because it could back up. The supplies were on rollers and we backed up, rolled the cargo out for a group of workers to handle and load on trucks, and the plane could be off again in just a few minutes. The government of Nigeria had a DC-4, which we called the Intruder. They rolled bombs out of its doors to try to discourage the relief effort, but the pilot stayed pretty high above small arms fire, so they were not very accurate. Still the relief planes didn't want to stay on the ground longer than necessary.

I was introduced to Tom Bellnap from Fresno, doing alternate service for the World Council of Churches. It was decided that I should stay with Tom for a few hours and go out with the last flight of the night to São Tomé. After we arrived, we drove around the airstrip for a while, supervising the unloading. Tom told me it was OK to take pictures, so I got one of a truck and workers unloading as well as a plane which had been bombed. I took a flash shot in the middle of the night of a plane unloading. The Biafran air force officer didn't like that I had taken the picture, and they took away my camera. Tom assured me that as soon as the officer had impressed everyone, the commissioner would give me back my camera. We followed a convoy of trucks to the storehouse six miles away. A storm broke out and a fallen tree blocked our way, so we had to go another route. At the storehouse I met a Kansan, a Swede, and two Dutchmen. They had been drinking, and I believed only about half of what they told me. I slept four hours on a mat on boards; then Tom awakened me and told me things were not going very well and it would be best if I got out of the country. We went back to the airstrip and I got out on a flight to São Tomé with one of Russ O'Quinn's captains. It was a beautiful flight. On the way I saw red streamers decorating the sky. I asked what they were, and they said, "Oh, they're shooting at us."

I slept until 1 00 p.m. and then went to the Biafra Counsel to seek approval to go in again and was told to be patient. I wrote that I was close to recommending that we not get involved for at least two reasons: 1) We're too late—others are already doing it. 2) And there was no good atmosphere for evangelizing and honoring Christ in the project. I was praying that the Christ who fed the five thousand would show me what to do in what looked like a hopeless situation.

I went to the Protestant church offices and met Tom, a former Peace Corps worker in Brazil. He drove me around the island, showed me a warehouse full of supplies, and to a place where Biafran children were being restored to health and then flown back to their parents. My roommate was real sick in the night, and I helped him get to a doctor. Tom and I talked to a Portuguese soldier who played with sharks like a bull fighter with bulls—and he had the scars to prove it, including one from an eel bite.

I waited for permission to go in again and talked to as many others as I could. I talked for an hour to a Biafran representative who had been to Syracuse University. I was convinced that the Biafra crisis needed a negotiated peace.

I found a flight that went direct from Cotonou to Basal, Switzerland, on Thursday, and was to be with Bob Pierce until Monday. Bob was there taking a Swiss treatment that was designed to restore his nervous system. He drove me around Switzerland before we left for Germany. From there I planned to fly to Paris, then London, and home.

On June 22, 1969, my family loaded up for a driving trip to Florida where I was to attend a convention. When we got close to Phoenix, we stopped to help a family with an overheated car, taking the woman to a service station. We stayed in a motel in Sun City that night. We went on to the Rio Grande and spent the night in El Paso, Texas, for $14. We went over the border into Juarez and back that night. The next night we were in Dallas. We went through beautiful country into Louisiana, a state none of us had been in before, and stopped at Baton Rouge on the banks of the Mississippi. Then driving through a tiny town called Bunkie, we were stopped by a local policeman who said I was driving too fast. He hauled us into city hall, and I had to pay $17, reduced from the original $27.

We went from there to New Orleans where I had to get the radio fixed. We swam in the motel pool, and in the evening went out for dinner. Afterward, we walked around, listening to music, and sat by the Mississippi watching the boats. It was so hot and humid, it was hard to sleep. The next day we headed east again along the Gulf Coast, enjoying the beautiful country. We stopped in Biloxi for drinks, then drove on to Mobile, Alabama, and Pensacola, Florida, where we stayed in a nice Rodeway Motel. I had to take the car in because it heated up, and got it fixed for $10. We got started after 1:00 p.m. and made our way down through Florida to Ocala where we stayed in our nicest hotel; probably through a mistake, it only cost $12. The next day, June 29, we made it to Miami Beach, checking in to a tenth floor room overlooking the ocean at the Sea Isle Hotel. We were attending a convention at which TV evangelist John Haggai gave the opening address. After attending several sessions, we drove down the Florida Keys, where Marcia and I were stung by little no-see-um bugs. We enjoyed some great skin diving and then went back to Miami Beach. I didn't find such a detailed account of our drive back home, but it was a memorable family driving trip.

In the next letter I found, I was on my way back to Asia on October 10, 1970. I was on a Japan Airlines 747 that was an hour late taking off from Los Angeles. There were many empty seats, so I could sleep some on the way. My brother-in-law, Floyd McClintick, who was in the Navy serving as recreation director at the naval air station, met me at the airport. He'd been able to get away in a nice Chevrolet station wagon to get me. That took some pull, and he wanted his sister to be impressed.

It was the first time Floyd had been in Tokyo for two years. I was wide awake by 2:00 a.m. We had waffles and got out to play golf by 8:00 a.m. He had a 10 handicap and mine was 15, so considering handicaps we tied. He shot 85, and I had an 89. We got his wife Etsuko at noon and went bowling. He beat me at that also, and Etsuko beat both of us. We went back for nine more holes of golf, and I beat him 45 to 47.

I took a train and taxi to the Tokyo airport where I was to meet Dr. Mooneyham, my boss, for a 6:20 p.m. flight to Korea, but he wasn't there. I learned from Joe Gooden, our World Vision man in Tokyo, that his plane out of Seattle had developed a fuel leak and turned back. We rescheduled and planned a 4:30 p.m. flight the next day. I checked into a room on the twelfth floor of the Otami Hotel and felt a scary earthquake.

I was in Bangkok, Thailand, on November 30 with Stan Mooneyham. It impressed me as a very busy, traffic-clogged city. I was amazed to see elephants on the streets. We stayed in a very fancy President Hotel where I went to the top floor and heard a great band. In Taipei, our host's niece was getting married in a Catholic ceremony. At the fifteen-course feast that followed, I was seated with one set of parents who kept piling food on my plate.

From Thailand, I went to Manila where the Cadds met me while they were on a two-week vacation. We had lots of time to talk, and they took me around the city and to Faith Academy (where later they named a new auditorium after them).

I went from there to Indonesia where I was leading an evangelistic thrust, partnering with five Indonesian evangelists and five expatriate speakers in five different cities. We had several meetings for training with good attendance until it rained, and fewer came. I was in a meeting with Peter Octavianos, a teacher in a World Evangelical Council school. His team had been reaching into Timor where the gospel had just been introduced. He told of a group who wanted to have communion but didn't have any wine. They had learned how Jesus turned the water into wine, so they prayed over some water, and on the eighth day it turned into wine. There were even stories of people raised from the dead, but I couldn't get confirmation of those stories.

From there I went to Singapore, probably my favorite place in Asia. I was fascinated with the small group/cell ministry which they did very well in one large church there. They ministered to several different ethnic groups with different languages, so the cell ministry was strategic.

On one trip with Dr. Mooneyham, we were to negotiate with some Vietnamese leaders in Paris. When we finished he said, "I don't like it here. Let's go to Majorca." We saw some bull fighting and jai alai, a game played with large, curved wicker baskets. That was my only visit to Spain.

On my last trip to Viet Nam, we visited President Key shortly before South Viet Nam fell. Interestingly, I was playing golf one day in Anaheim in about 2010 and was put with an Asian man and his wife. When he told me his name was Key, I said I had visited a President of Viet Nam named Key. He said, "That was me." He lived near us off Katella Avenue.

Northwest Yearly Meeting

In 1971 I received an invitation to become superintendent of Northwest Yearly Meeting of Friends
Church—the Friends churches in Oregon, Washington,
and Idaho. I had enjoyed my work with World Vision,
but as Mary and I prayed about it, we had a surprising but firm sense that I should accept that invitation.
World Vision threw a great farewell party for me, and
I remember Dr. Mooneyham saying that they should
be proud to be able to send skilled workers to serve
the church. So we moved to Newberg in late summer.
They built a house for us and provided me with a new
Chrysler. I remember sitting in my back yard, reading
at 9:00 p.m., surprised that it was light so late.

In June 1971, I made a trip to South America
to set up pastors conferences for World Vision,
and having been invited to be superintendent of
Northwest Yearly Meeting, I used that trip to visit
Friends missions in Bolivia on the way. I wrote
home on June 10 that I'd had an eight-hour flight on
Varig to Lima. World Vision staff member Bill Kent
was to meet me there, but his wife was in the hospital, so he couldn't; he had arranged for me to fly
first class to La Paz, even though I had an economy

ticket. Friends missionaries, the Comforts and the Thomases, met me at the airport and took me in a Volkswagen bus to where I was to stay. I wrote that it was cold in La Paz at thirteen thousand feet. I had some altitude sickness until they gave me some medication and told me to breathe deeply, and that helped. We talked for a couple of hours, I rested, and we ate. The next day we took a two-hour drive on the dirt Pan American Highway to the border of Peru, where we shared a picnic lunch with Friends missionaries working in Peru. I remember marveling that the missionary children could run and play in that altitude without becoming exhausted. Of course, they had grown up in that altitude and their lungs were expanded. I went out in the country to see a TEE (Theological Education by Extension) class in operation. There were a teacher and two students, four pigs, and two burros. The next day we went an hour and a half out onto the Altiplano to go to Sunday school and a church meeting. I spoke through two interpreters.

After I left Bolivia and felt free from censorship, I wrote that President Torres was very weak, and they expected a revolution at any time. The Peace Corps had been told they had ninety days to get out, but suddenly had to leave earlier. Missionaries had plans for quick withdrawals. I once heard there had been revolutions in Bolivia about once a year.

On one trip, I visited the mission work of California Friends in Chiquimula, Guatemala. Missionary John Astleford drove me from Chiquimula back to Guatemala City and on the way recounted the story of the time he was driving to Guatemala City, and he picked up a hitch hiker who shot him. He shoved John down on the passenger side floor thinking he was dead. John said, "I thought, 'Be still and know that I am God.'" For some reason his attacker drove off the road just short of Guatemala City and walked away, leaving the keys in the ignition. John waited for a few minutes to be sure he was gone, and then with God-given strength was able to drive into the city to the hospital where his life was saved. His brother who lived on the Oregon coast was awakened that morning with the urgent feeling that he should pray for his brother in Guatemala.

I flew from Bolivia to Sao Paulo, Brazil, where I had an hour and a half layover, then on to Porto Alegre where two men from the pastors conference committee met me. We talked for a while, and then I was on my own. It was thirty-seven degrees outside, and they didn't have heat in most of the buildings, so I went out to buy something warm. I went to a movie with English subtitles—a good way to learn the language. I got so I could almost make sense of newspaper articles. A taxi driver told me there were eight million people in Sao Paulo and the average income was $40 a month.

The next day I went to a Lutheran pastors meeting; there were six hundred thousand Lutherans in Brazil. I then went to a Methodist bishop's office, and we went over plans for the conference. I also spoke to pastors from the Porta Alegre area. Then I made plans to go to Santiago; I was trying to get there early, but it was not a good trip. An Argentine Airline flight was canceled, so I went to the Porta Alegre airport by 6:30 p.m. for an 8:45 flight on a Cruzero (Brazilian) plane. I waited in a freezing airport until midnight because there was too much fog to fly. I was fighting a cold, which the weather didn't help. We had a one-hour flight, and I got to my hotel at 3:00 a.m. The next morning, we flew to Cordoba where World Vision had held a pastors conference in 1962, then on to Mendoza. After a wait, we took off for a short flight to Santiago but had to turn back—about forty minutes later we were back in Mendoza. We had gone through pockets of the roughest air I had ever experienced flying over the Andes. We waited from 5:00 until 7:00 p.m. in a restaurant then were told our airline would not try again until 4:20 p.m. the next day. When we learned that a Chilean airline was leaving at about 9:00, we all transferred. It took off at 10:00. By going over a lower part of the Andes, it took about twenty minutes longer and the crew stayed belted in the whole way, but we made it. Four men waited for us at the airport from 4:00 until 10:00 p.m., and they took me to an old but fine Pan American Hotel. I wrote home that traveling is not always a bed of roses, but I was doing this for Jesus, so it is worthwhile.

Later, though I had already left World Vision to be superintendent of Northwest Yearly Meeting, World Vision asked me to join the pastors conference team that was going to conduct the meetings I had set up. Dr. Paul Rees, director of the conference, had had a heart procedure and could not go. I wrote home on October 11, 1971, that things looked good for our conference (our fourth) in Columbia. There were 650 registered.

We had already had three conferences on that trip—one of which was in Granada. Dr. Dick Halverson, leader of that team, was a long-time member of the World Vision board, then pastor of the Fourth Presbyterian Church in Washington DC, and later chaplain of the Senate. He and Dave Morken and I had a very helpful evening together. Each of us had sons who had rebelled, and Dick's son, Steve, had come back to the Lord. He said there was little we could do except pray, and it was unlikely I would be the one to bring my son back. Dick made relationships high on his priority list: first his relationship with God, second his relationship with family, and third his relationship with his work team. Late in his ministry he had learned that he needed to move relationship with family higher in his priorities. One day his wife had said, "Honey, when you say 'we' you don't mean 'us' anymore." And she was right. As superintendent, I had just moved from subordinate positions to a leadership role, and I decided I also needed to strengthen my family priority.

I preached in an Episcopal church on Sunday morning in Bogota. I remember that in one of those conference sessions, Dick Halverson was speaking, and he told the story of a time when Armin Gesswein, founder of Revival Prayer Fellowship, had been with friends in New York, and they came to Grand Central Station to see him off. They had talked about Romans 12:1–2. After they left, Armin thought to himself that he had read and memorized Romans 12:1–2, "Present your bodies a living sacrifice…" but he was not sure he had ever really done it. With his shoe, he marked a cross on the floor of the station, stood on that cross, and presented his body. Dick asked the pastors to make a cross at their feet, kneel on that cross, and present their bodies. They fell on their knees and began to all pray at once as they do in many countries—at first a mumble, then growing into a mighty crescendo unto the Lord.

I served as superintendent of Northwest Yearly Meeting from the summer of 1971 until 1979. I did not spend as much time traveling, so I didn't write letters detailing my life. And without letters, my account of that part of my career won't be extensive.

There were sixty Friends churches in Oregon, Washington, and Idaho. We grew by about 3 percent during my tenure, which doesn't seem like much, but it was not a time of much church growth across America. Our finances were healthy. I hired Quentin Nordyke, a distant relative, as my assistant. We had a secretary and a treasurer in the office. It was during those days I supervised the transition to computers. My experience with computers to that point had just been that I knew World Vision had a big one housed in a room at a certain temperature. Now we could have desktop computers—which didn't seem to make our work easier or quicker but helped in the long run.

I gave a keynote message at each of our annual yearly meetings, and I became aware that God was leading me to themes that were prominent among other Christian leaders across the country. One year, Mary and I moved to Boise Valley, Idaho, to be near the churches in that area. We rented a place and stayed there for several months.

One night in May 1973, I received a call from a member of our Seattle Friends church, telling me that if we didn't approve and credential a pastor from the Nazarene church who was divorced, his church would withdraw from the yearly meeting. That night I passed out in the bathroom from a bleeding ulcer and was taken to Newberg Community Hospital for several days. I remember that after not eating for a few days they served me asparagus soup, and that has been my favorite soup ever since. Later we learned of research that found a bacterium was more responsible for ulcer problems than was stress. I took a simple treatment to kill that bacteria and have had no trouble since.

During this time, I was struggling with an allergy problem that caused me to swell in different parts of my body. About three times I went to emergency rooms because swelling in my throat made it hard to breathe. Once I was in the hospital for six days. They decided I was allergic to many things in the air more than to things I ate.

In a meeting of the spiritual oversight committee, we dealt with the question of whether to approve that divorced Nazarene pastor for ministry in a Friends church. In that meeting we had a quiet time to wait on the Lord for his wisdom. I remember I sensed a clear message from the Lord, "Be still and see the mercy of the Lord." I knew then that I didn't need to lobby for a certain outcome, only wait to see what the Lord would do. We approved his ministry, and he served one of our churches successfully for many years.

During my tenure as superintendent, I led a conference of Friends in Denver with Ralph Winter of the U.S. Center for World Missions in Pasadena as our speaker. I knew my service as superintendent was coming to an end, and I asked if he thought my wife and I should now offer to serve as missionaries. We had long told the Lord we were ready to go anywhere and do anything. Ralph said, "No, I think you would serve well as a link between the church and missions." That felt to me like a word from the Lord and helped me to know that I should later accept the invitation of Dr. Ted Engstrom, vice president of World Vision, to return to World Vision as director of church relations.

New Call to Peacemaking

The Viet Nam war ended during my term as superintendent. We knew that we were living in a very dangerous world because of nuclear proliferation. I felt that the followers of the Prince of Peace should have more to offer to a world caught in the tragic threat of the nuclear age than just, "I won't fight." I felt that what we in the peace churches had done in the past was not adequate in a nuclear age. War was not working. The solution to the threat we faced was not to kill more people—God must have a better solution, and if war is wrong, what is right? There never was a time when war was less popular. There never was a time when war was more destructive. In a paper titled "The Arms Race or the Human Race," E. Raymond Wilson pointed out that the world's military spending in 1975 was about $300 billion. There were almost twenty-six million men and women in military service worldwide, at a cost of $12,350 per person per year, while we were spending just $219 a year to train a school-age child. The Friends Committee on National Legislation said the nuclear stockpile in the United States was then equal to six hundred fifteen thousand Hiroshima bombs. We could destroy every Russian city with a population of over one hundred thousand more than thirty-six times, and Russia had enough nuclear weapons to destroy our cities nine times. The money spent in the United States Defense Department in just five days would double what we were paying to assist developing countries in a year.

At an annual national meeting of Friends superintendents, I voiced my concern. They felt that an initiative like I was proposing should be carried by as large a part of the church as possible. When I was in Paris, I spoke with the Billy Graham Association representative, and he helped me get in touch with officials who were planning the 1974 Lausanne Conference on Evangelization. I wrote to some of them about my concern and received some meaningful answers—one from the editor of *Christianity Today* magazine, and one from Billy Graham's son-in-law, Leighton Ford. Arthur John Dain, who was in charge of planning the program, said the peacemaking theme was too controversial, too time consuming, and too far from the main theme to be considered at that conference. When I shared that at the next superintendents meeting they said, "Then we must do it ourselves."

We sought for an answer to the threat of nuclear war that was spiritually based and so sound, so positive, so practical, and so contemporary that it would attract peace-loving people to a common, productive effort. We soon felt that it should be broader than just among Friends, so we shared the concept with leaders of the Mennonite Central Committee and with leaders of the Brethren Church, and they joined wholeheartedly. We had a meeting in Washington DC with the Russian ambassador, and one with Henry Kissinger. We planned and conducted twenty-seven regional conferences and one national conference at Green Lake, Wisconsin, held October 5–8, 1978. Out of that conference we issued a "New Call to Peacemaking," which we tried to communicate as broadly as possible. That conference was covered in the *Christianity Today* magazine and in the December 4 *Newsweek* magazine. We found that there was strong support for peace at that time. The Catholic church had a strong peace movement, as did the Baptist church, the Methodist church, and many others. At that time Senator Mark Hatfield of Oregon and Senator Hartke of Indiana introduced a bill to establish a George Washington Peace Academy in the tradition of the military academies. I found a May 1979 letter from President Jimmy Carter thanking us for our kind words about his efforts to bring a peace settlement in the Middle East.

I edited and wrote the introduction to a small book titled, *The New Call to Peacemaking: A Challenge to All Friends*, which was used as a resource guide for those conferences. In my introduction I told of my experience in Monrovia, Liberia, when the Organization for African Unity was trying to negotiate a peace agreement between the central government of Nigeria and the Biafra contingent. I wrote of my forty-five minutes with the head of the Biafra delegation, the chief justice of their supreme court, trying to find out what it would take for them to settle peaceably. I got the impression that, as in many conflicts, there was a breakdown in communications. I told how that war ended when the Biafran General Ojukwu was deposed. Over two million people had died. Some who claimed to know that situation have said that the Methodist president of Nigeria at that time had no intention of destroying the Ibo tribe people, and if better communication could have revealed that, many lives might have been saved. The emphasis on peacemaking was more popular under some presidents than under others. The movement continued for several years, last led by John Stoner of the Mennonite Central Committee.

World Vision Again

It was in 1979 that I was invited to return to World Vision as director of church relations, and I felt very comfortable accepting that position. I felt good that I had left World Vision honorably enough to be invited back. We bought a condo on Foothill and Magnolia in Monrovia. Our son, David, lived there later while we were living in Arvada, Colorado, and I owned it until he died in 2007.

As director of church relations, I helped to coordinate Managing Your Time seminars, developed and taught by Dr. Ted Engstrom and Ed Dayton. I was also made director of prayer ministry, and in that capacity became a part of the National Prayer Committee in the early 1980s. Vonette Bright of Campus Crusade was the chair, and Dick Eastman and Evelyn Christianson were members. Glenn Shepard of the Southern Baptist church came on when I did. We planned an American Festival of Evangelism Prayer Congress in September 1980. I coordinated a national week of prayer from May 31– June 7, 1981. We urged pastors to preach on prayer and keep their church doors open to praying people that week. The American Festival of Evangelism was held in Kansas City, July 27–30, 1981. Billy Graham was the concluding speaker, and when that conference was over, we petitioned the Lausanne committee to let us continue as the National Prayer Committee, and that was granted. There were only about ten of us on the committee at first, then it grew to about eighty. I served as secretary for over thirty years and was vice-chair for a while.

We sponsored the National Day of Prayer, which led a prayer meeting in the senate office building in Washington every year and at this writing has promoted over forty-five thousand prayer meetings across the country on the first Thursday of May each year. Presidents had called for a National Day of Prayer every year since the Truman era, but we never knew when it would be, so we couldn't prepare or promote it effectively. Vonette Bright appealed to President Reagan who agreed to put it on the same day every year, even though Congress had decided there would be no more special days. I was in a meeting when the Secretary of the Interior said, "I wish I had Vonette Bright on my team. I never saw anything go through Congress like the National Day of Prayer." We also had prayer summits in various cities where we taught on prayer and led concerts of prayer.

In August 1980, I made an orientation trip to seven nations of Asia. In the Philippines, we made an hour-and-a-half trip by pontoon boat to several islands where we saw development evangelism in action. In India we visited an area near Madras which was known as the "graveyard of missions."

They had seen seven hundred baptisms in the previous two years. We spent nearly an hour with Mother Teresa of Calcutta, just after she received the Nobel Peace Prize. Her Missionaries of Charity had a home for abandoned babies and a home where poor people could die with dignity. They were feeding seven thousand people every day and cared for fifty-two thousand victims of leprosy. We asked her how we could pray for them, and she said, "Pray that we may be more holy; that we may understand the purity of life and the community of life." She warned me not to go out in the heat of the afternoon. On that trip we noted especially the effectiveness of development evangelism.

In September, maybe 1981 or 1982, we took a vacation trip to Europe. We rented a little Renault in Paris which got thirty-eight miles per gallon and drove that day to the border with Germany. In four countries we visited, there was no speed limit on freeways, and I was sure some were passing us at a 100 miles per hour at least. We drove toward Salzburg and visited Oberammergau, saw a Ludwig castle, and got to our timeshare in St. Johann, about sixty kilometers south of Salzburg. I played golf a couple of times. One day we went and saw the birth place of Mozart. We drove through Austria to Trento, Italy, then to our next timeshare resort at six-thousand-foot elevation. We stopped to view the wonderful scenery, and my camera was stolen from our car while we were just a few feet away. We drove from there to Venice and took a boat from the mainland. We had tea in St. Mark's Square under the shadow of a great church while listening to a great orchestra. I wanted to ride the gondolas, but they were charging tourists $80, and I thought that was robbery. We drove the next day to a town on the border of Monaco and stayed right on the Mediterranean. The next day we stopped briefly at Monte Carlo and drove almost five hundred miles to the edge of Paris. On our last Sunday we went out to see the palace at Versailles and saw the Louvre. We flew back to Los Angeles the next day.

Our Christmas letter in 1983 said that my work at World Vision had taken me to San Antonio, Texas, to help with a project, and that I was speaker for a World Gospel Mission annual retreat in Santa Cruz, Bolivia. In 1984 we had an International Prayer Assembly at the Young Nak Presbyterian Church in Seoul, Korea, with over four thousand in attendance from seventy countries. While we were praying together, more than one thousand Koreans were praying in a nearby park, sometimes in the rain. I taught a class on "Hindrances to Prayer." Many of us went to Hong Kong and took a boat into China. I remember learning that there was considerable interest in capitalism and thinking that if all the people who rode bicycles ever got cars, there would be a big traffic problem. We had an evening meal in a big restaurant and used that occasion to have a communion service. As we left, the staff who served us followed us out to our bus to bid us farewell.

While working at World Vision full time, I was asked to serve as interim pastor of the Friends Church at Bell. The interim lasted for eight years, ending in 1987. I was mostly just a Sunday pastor. Fern Cottone was my secretary and helped with a lot of the pastoral duties during the week. She later moved to Quaker Gardens and was instrumental in getting management to invite me to be chaplain. After I was replaced as pastor at Bell Friends, I was invited back on September 27 to lead a memorial service for a member. That was the Sunday we got an early call from our son-in-law Wes Voth, telling us that our daughter Marilyn had died in the night. I took David with me and conducted the service but have wondered if anything might have been different if I had still been pastor there and had the prayers of the saints at that church supporting our family. Her death was a complete shock. Even Wes had no reason to expect it. As far as we could tell, she was under a great deal of pressure in her doctoral program, and because she'd had rheumatic fever as a child, her heart couldn't handle it. She was at the top of her class of seven hundred students. They had appointed her as a student teacher. Her thesis was so outstanding they published it. Wes had her ashes spread over the University of Hawaii garden. Out of that tragic loss, I wrote the little tract I called *The Ultimate Answer to the Why Question,* which has ministered to many over the years since.

In 1987 I helped, along with Ben Jennings of Campus Crusade and Armin Gesswein of Revival Prayer Fellowship, to lead a tour in the Holy Land to sites where significant prayer events took place in Bible times. It was a traveling prayer seminar. We taught at each place how the experience of that trip could help enhance our prayer life. Len Rogers who had started the Youth for Christ ministry in the Holy Land and lived there for many years, introduced us to the Christian church of the Middle East. We learned better how to support them and help bear their burdens.

Before I left my second season at World Vision after thirteen years, I was made assistant to the director of the U.S. ministries. We sponsored Love, Inc., an effort to help churches minister to the poor. I wrote a memo to administrators on World Vision's prayer ministry. I wrote that there was considerable evidence that God was orchestrating a significant, growing, worldwide prayer movement. It had a two-fold focus: prayer for spiritual awakening in the church and prayer for worldwide evangelization. I said one of the main reasons we should bathe our ministry in prayer was that our humanitarian services had given us an entrée into some of the previously closed cultures, and to be good stewards of the opportunities afforded us, we needed all the spiritual dynamic available. To illustrate how World Vision was using its influence in the prayer movement, I pointed out that under David Bryant's leadership in Chicago, a group had launched the Concerts of Prayer movement, similar to those under Jonathan Edwards, which brought the First Great Awakening in our country. I started the San Gabriel Valley Concert of Prayer which continued to be one of the strongest concerts in the country. I also helped start the Southern California Concerts of Prayer and served as its chair. David Bryant eventually left his position at Intervarsity to head the Concert of Prayer movement and asked me to serve on his board. I was also chair of the board of Armin Gesswein's Revival Prayer Fellowship.

When I left, I had been with World Vision longer than any other employee—twenty-eight years. They put on a very gracious "Tribute to Norval Hadley" chapel on April 8, 1992.

Evangelical Friends Mission

In April 1992, I accepted the invitation to be executive
director of Evangelical Friends Mission, the international mission organization of evangelical Friends.
It sponsored mission work in Mexico; Rwanda, Africa;
India; the Navajo Reservation around Rough Rock;
the Philippines; Ireland; and an international student
ministry out of Texas. It was supported by all the
yearly meetings in the Evangelical Friends Alliance
(now Evangelical Friends Church-North America),
although EFM didn't try to become the administrator
of all evangelical Friends mission work. Eastern
Region supported EFM but had its own work in India,
Taiwan, Hong Kong, and other places. Mid-America
Yearly Meeting had work in Burundi but also supported
EFM. Rocky Mountain Yearly Meeting had turned its
mission among the Navajo over to EFM. Northwest
Yearly Meeting had work in Bolivia and also supported
EFM. So while EFM didn't control all the evangelical
Friends mission work, we wanted to help create unity
by soliciting prayer and providing information on all
the mission fields. While I was director, California
Yearly Meeting left its association with Friends United
Meeting and joined EFC-NA. They continued to

administer their own mission programs in Central America and Alaska but became strong supporters of EFM, and that greatly strengthened our mission ministry.

We moved to Arvada, Colorado, on the western edge of Denver on April 25. I continued to be part of the National Prayer Committee. We had breakfast with President George H. W. Bush on the National Day of Prayer that year and one other year. I served on the boards of Global Recordings International, Concerts of Prayer International, and Steve Cadd's Sword Productions. At one time I served on seven boards. I was also vice president and administrator of Venture International, a ministry led by Len Rodgers in the Middle East. That ministry sent Mary and me to Cyprus for a "Signs of Hope" conference, a project of Evangelicals for Middle East Understanding. We toured Syria, Jordan, and Israel on that trip and spent time in London on the way home. I went to Cairo, Egypt, in February 1992 to help Jim Neal, former World Vision staff member and then vice president of Youth for Christ, lead two Managing Your Time seminars for leaders of the Middle East Council of Churches. We rode camels by the pyramids. In September of that year the Four Flats Quartet got together in Newberg to sing for the George Fox University centennial celebration. When I announced in a letter on April 10 that I was moving to a new position I wrote, "I believe God is doing something special these days toward giving everyone a chance to decide whether or not to make Christ Lord, and it seems right that we are moving to the front lines of that movement."

George H. W. Bush and I at the National Day of Prayer.

To Norval Hadley
with best wishes, Geo Bush

The National Prayer Committee along with
George H. W. and Barbara Bush.

In May 1987, on my way home from the National Day of Prayer observance in Washington DC, I stopped in Ohio where leaders of the New Call to Peacemaking were meeting with the Baptist Peace Fellowship. Out of that meeting came the proposal that we call for the year 2000 to be a Year of Peace. We wanted Christians everywhere to celebrate the two-thousandth birthday of the Prince of Peace by calling war factions to a moratorium on fighting at least for that year—and we offered ourselves to help plan and implement that moratorium. We proposed that resources not needed for violence be redirected to help meet human need. This proposal was adopted by the Baptist World Alliance meeting in Amman, Jordan, the following July and by several other denominational bodies. It was presented to the United Nations International Conference on Relationship between Disarmament and Development. It was distributed to the members of that conference when they met from August 24–September 11, 1987, urging that we enter the third millennium free from the threat of war, and that we focus during that year on exploring nonviolent forms of conflict resolution.

On one of my first visits as director of Evangelical Friends Mission, I wrote from Mexico City in September 1992 that the work in that predominantly Catholic society was very difficult. Many convert but don't stick to it. We didn't have enough national workers. Our oldest and nicest church had a beautiful building but only eleven people attending regularly; other groups met in homes. Our missionaries in Mexico City were often sick. The work in Mexico City had been started a few years earlier by Roscoe Knight, a former missionary to Bolivia, the first mission project of Evangelical Friends Mission. There was another Mexican mission near the California border started by California Friends. We brought the two together as the beginning of a Mexico Yearly Meeting, and I was delighted to see that they had great fellowship together.

During my tenure as director of Evangelical Friends Mission, there was devastating conflict in Rwanda. I wrote home in February 1993 that at midnight on February 7, two hundred rebel troops launched an attack in the north of Rwanda in the worst fighting since 1959. People from several cities fled for their lives. Rebels took our church in Kidaho (near the Uganda border) as their headquarters. One lady said she had seen the bodies of twenty of our church members who had been killed there. Our Friends pastor had been away, taking his wife to the hospital in Kigali, when the attack took place; he was back and still looking for his four children when I wrote. The director of our Friends school and several of his staff were in rebel hands. One survivor told our pastor that the rebels rounded up about three thousand people in the market area, telling them that they would take care of them, and then threw grenades into the crowd. After Rwandan troops drove the rebels farther north, our churches and schools became housing for refugees. When I wrote, our missionaries had been placed in the first stage of the American Embassy's evacuation plan, but we decided they should stay until the second stage. The United States ambassador said he knew of at least nine hundred thousand refugees. I wrote that it may have been just the tip of the iceberg, which turned out to be true, for just about a year later, Rwanda was engulfed in genocide.

I wrote home in October 1992 from Manila. I was there to try to help resolve a conflict between our director, Jaime and a pastor there. I had some good time during that trip with the Cadds. They had a friend get me on the golf course just across from their condo. I had time for only twelve holes with a caddy, but it was a good experience.

I went from there to India where EFM had sent the Hunerwadel family to plant a church among the Garhwali, an unreached people group. I was there October 22–30, 1992. Carl Hunerwadel met me at the Delhi airport with a taxi in which he had driven down from Mussoorie, which was a resort area at about seven-thousand-foot altitude—much cooler than most of India. Carl taught at Woodstock School just above Mussoorie. They had two flat tires on the way down to Delhi, and we had two more on our way back. It was an eight-hour trip. It was interesting to see monkeys along the road. The temperature got down into the thirties at night. I took a kerosene heater and a suitcase full of gifts and medicines.

The thing that impressed me was the Hunerwadel family. We got up at 6:00 a.m., and devotions were from 6:15 until 7:00. Every child had a Bible as they sat around the dining table. They read first an Old Testament portion, then from the New Testament, the Psalm of the day, and a Proverb. They were reading through the Bible in a year. Then they sang the hymn of the month, and each child prayed. I had met a family in Paonia, Colorado, where Hunerwadels had lived, who were going through the Bible with them and singing the same hymns. After breakfast, Carl slipped off to school, and Peggy got the three youngest children started on their home-school assignments, then excused herself because she always spent the next hour in prayer. She put on a one-hour tape of Christian instrumental music and prayed until it was done. I asked if I could join her. I was amazed that the children didn't even talk to each other while she was praying. A veteran missionary said the Garhwali love families. We felt God had indeed sent this family to them.

Woodstock School had over four hundred students from all over the world, though most were from India. It offered high quality education and had hundreds of applications for only one hundred openings per year. Carl taught music and organized a musical witness to the community, though he was warned that non-Christian parents might object. They took twenty children from their expatriate Kellogg Church to do musical evangelism in Delhi for a week.

A young student who converted from Hinduism witnessed to thousands of Hindus. A Bible study started in the Hunerwadel home would become the first Garhwali church. Edwin, the Garhwali assistant pastor of the Kellogg Church, was going out to villages for four days twice a month to witness. A year before, he had been expelled from a village, and his guitar was taken from him when he tried to witness, but now, in answer to prayer, they were more free to witness. There were seven million people scattered across those hills, most of whom had never heard of Jesus. Carl and Peggy were planning to spend their winter break in the village though they could not speak the language of the people, so I took them two tapes in the Garhwali language from Global Recordings. Our eight-hour trip back to Delhi on a small chartered bus took thirteen hours. We had another flat tire and a broken spring this time.

I met John Williams, superintendent of the Evangelical Friends Church—Eastern Region, at the Delhi airport, and we took a plane to Chhatarpur where his region had sponsored a mission program for many years. We flew over Agra where the Taj Mahal is, which I saw only from the air. From the time we arrived until we left, there were people lined up to talk to John about problems and questions, most relating to power struggles in the early months of the first absence of Anglo missionaries. We started our time there by calling all the principals to an extended time of prayer, and we saw God answer prayer. One bright spot was the work of an evangelist who went out from the hospital and had over a hundred converts or seekers from surrounding villages who met with them every month.

I went from India to Hong Kong with John Williams on October 30, 1992. Dave and Cindy Aufrance were missionaries under the Evangelical Friends Church—Eastern Region. David gave us a tour of Hong Kong by bus, train, tram, taxi, and ferry. Hong Kong had 247,500 people per square mile (New York had only 11,480). The Hong Kong government was the largest landlord in the world. Fifty percent of the people, or three million, rented from the government. I figured the government took in about $750 million a month in rent. As a result, the slums were virtually eliminated. Instead, high-rise buildings were everywhere. David was director of the One Mission Society work in Hong Kong. They had the United Christian School with 1,081 students from first grade through two years of junior college. Ninety percent of their expenses were paid by the government. All the teachers were Christians who prayed for their students. Fifteen percent were Christian when they came, but 70 percent when they left. There were at least fourteen OMS churches in the area.

I served the Evangelical Friends Mission until the year 2000. I discovered I had type 2 diabetes in 1998, and it became difficult to control well while on the road. I tried retirement, but I was not very good at it. I had enjoyed playing golf since I was about twenty. There was a time when I had back trouble, and it took me three days to recover from a round of golf, but God graciously took that away. I've had four holes in one, and the director who hired me at Quaker Gardens, Michael Gamet, considered me his golf mentor. We discovered that the Orange County Senior Olympics did not include golf, and we got them to do so. Golfers compete just against people in their five-year age group. I've now won seven gold medals in the Southern California Senior Olympic games, though I have to admit that the last three years no one else in my age group showed up. Michael talked me into going to St. George, Utah, to compete in the Huntsman World Senior Games. I won bronze (third place). That got me an invitation to the Nationals, and he went with me to Houston as my caddy. Many of the guys I played against from the Carolinas and Florida were par golfers just a few years ago, so I didn't win anything, but it was an honor to compete in the Nationals. I have shot my age every year since I was 74 and shot 72. I think golf has helped me keep my blood sugar level down and maybe extended my life.

A gift from Northwest Friends Church Arvada, CO when I retired as Director of EFM.

Quaker Gardens/
Rowntree Gardens

When I retired, I wasn't satisfied to just play golf and lay around, so I got a job driving for a funeral home, which I had done just out of high school. Then when I got an invitation to be chaplain at Quaker Gardens, a senior living community in sunny California, I was glad to accept. They moved us into the nicest house on their campus and in six years I had earned my way in as a Lifecare Resident. I planned the Sunday services, led Bible studies and prayer meetings, and tried to visit everyone who went to the hospital. I preached three or four times a year, but we had some of the best preachers and musicians come—retired ministers, professors and nationally known leaders. Because most of our residents were near the end of their life, I felt we were living on the threshold of heaven and felt a keen responsibility to help residents get ready for that transition. My son, David, died of cancer in 2007 at age fifty-five, and my wife, Mary, died of colitis in 2010.

Carol Rosenberger and I got married August 12, 2012. She had moved into Quaker Gardens in 2010 with her husband, Richard, who had heart trouble, and after just a few months, he passed away. She came to my Bible studies and prayer meetings, so we became friends. One day she "eldered" me for always sitting at the same table at meals—I was the chaplain, and I should move around. After that I would look to see where she was sitting and join her. One time when the people at our table were talking about restaurants and eating out I said, "I like to go out to breakfast every Monday morning." Carol said, "I like to go out for breakfast." I thought, "Great! Now maybe the servers won't think I don't have any friends."

After going out for breakfast a few Mondays, I had a dream that I was married to Carol. I remembered that my boss, Dr. Pierce, used to say, "God leads his dear children along; me he jerks." I wondered if God was jerking me toward this wonderful lady, but I wrestled with how to find out. One breakfast she was talking about her previous marriage, and I blurted out, "Do you think you would ever want to be married again?" And she told me all the reasons she would never want to be married again, so we decided to just be friends. Then the next Thursday she took me to the Art-A-Fair at the Laguna Beach Festival of Arts to show me where she displayed and sold her art work. We had a good time. The next day she wanted to go out to Taco Bell for a coke, her great extravagance. We would go only during happy hour when cokes only cost $1. There she said, "The real answer to your question is: I wouldn't want to be married again unless I could be married to you." That did it. We went right out and bought a ring.

We went to pre-marital counseling with her pastor, Gary Drabek of the Springdale Baptist Church in Westminster. After the second session he said, "Oh, you guys know more about this than I do," and graduated us. We were married in a small, private, invitation-only wedding on a Sunday afternoon in his church. We went away for a short honeymoon to the Welk resort, and Community Services Director Randy Wayamori put a note in everyone's box saying we were married. When we got back we had a great reception. I felt like a wonderful spirit of love spread across the whole campus.

Carol graduated from Stanford University as an art major. Her father and older brother, Dick, also graduated from Stanford. Dick is now a country doctor in Georgia. Her younger brother, Ed, is a professional photographer and a photography professor in Utah. She is the daughter of a prominent physician who had an office on Hadley Street in Whittier, California. She had done a beautiful drawing of the Hadley house. Her mother was an art teacher at Whittier High School before she was married. She taught with Pat Nixon. Her grandfather was also a physician there during the Depression and was often paid with chickens and avocados. Her great grandfather was a Friends missionary to Ramallah, Jordan, and became president of William Penn College in Oskaloosa, Iowa, and president of Whittier College. I felt like I had married up. Carol had received training in personal evangelism and has been a great help to me as we visited in hospitals. Several residents have come to the Lord. We have had a happy marriage and life together.

Quaker Gardens hired a branding company to try to find the best ways to attract new residents. They determined that the word Quaker made us sound too old fashioned and exclusive, so they changed the name to Rowntree Gardens, named after a Quaker philanthropist in England who served seniors. Serving as chaplain at Rowntree Gardens felt like a most fitting way to conclude my career. After fifteen years in that position there was some question if I should be driving to hospitals at age ninety, and my hearing made it hard to be a good counselor, so we decided it was time to retire again. I could keep busy at least for a while writing my memoirs.

It has been a wonderful, adventurous career. Soon after I felt called to Christian ministry, I determined that I wanted more than anything else to live in the center of God's will. Thus the verses in 1 John 5:14–15 have been important to me, "Now this is the confidence that we have in Him, that if we ask anything according to His will, He hears us. And if we know that He hears us, whatever we ask, we know that we have the petitions that we have asked of Him." There can't be any prayer that is more according to his will than the prayer: Lord, let me have your will. So I knew that if I could pray that prayer out of a surrendered heart (Romans 12:1–2), God would guide me. Thus, I have lived my life with the assurance that whatever trouble God allowed to come my way, it was OK, even if it led me to my home in heaven.

A wedding picture of Carol and me.

Carol's drawing of the Hadley house in Whittier, California.

Two pictures from my retirement party from
chaplaincy at Rowntree Gardens

www.ingramcontent.com/pod-product-compliance
Lightning Source LLC
La Vergne TN
LVHW041302080426
835510LV00009B/840